HOW TO
FLOURISH
IN A
FALLEN WORLD

HOW TO FLOURISH

IN A
FALLEN WORLD

BY
DR. DONALD DEMARCO

EN ROUTE BOOKS & MEDIA

ENROUTE

En Route Books & Media

Back cover background image "dead forest" by Matt MacGillivray, Flickr
Creative Commons adapted and changed by T.J. Burdick
https://flic.kr/p/dNBWf

Back cover additional image "All Green and Final" by Paul Ferguson, Flickr
Creative Commons adapted and changed by T.J. Burdick
https://flic.kr/p/8BLyDf

Front cover image "Lone Pine in a tree Farm" by Charles Knowles, Flickr
Creative Commons adapted and changed by T.J. Burdick
https://flic.kr/p/bKj2nF

© 2015, En Route Books & Media,
5705 Rhodes Avenue, St. Louis, MO 63109
Contact us at contactus@enroutebooksandmedia.com

Print ISBN: 978-1-950108-65-7
E-book ISBN: 978-1-63337-042-5

ACKNOWLEDGEMENTS

Many streams of thought enter the mind of an author, providing the fodder and the formula for a book. I am indebted to more people, places, events, and experiences than I can possibly recount. They remain in my debt, unnamed, but not un-cherished. Also in my debt are the editors of *The Human Life Review, The Hartford Catholic Transcript, Voices, The National Catholic Register, Social Justice Review, Homiletic & Pastoral Review, Crisis, Interim, The Wanderer, Celebrate Life, Linacre,* and *This Rock.*

—Dedication—

This book is prayerfully dedicated to our grandchildren with the ardent hope that they will flourish despite the fallen world in which they must find their way.

Dr. Donald DeMarco
September 25, 2014
Kirchener, Ontario

CONTENTS

FOREWORD

Dr. DeMarco's book comes just ten years after another book (co-authored with Benjamin Wiker) entitled *The Architects of the Culture of Death*. That previous book was a response, as he says, to the question raised by the then Pope John Paul II (now canonized) in his encyclical "The Gospel of Life": "How did this situation come about?" This new book is a response to the question that follows naturally upon that one: "How do we cope with the dreadful situation, this culture of death, we (i.e. the whole world) are faced with?"

The Church has in fact given the answer from the time of Christ – it is nothing but the message of salvation. That is the key to the culture of Life. However, the message has had to be reiterated time and time again, for every age. The message is one of love, such love as God had for fallen mankind that the Father sent his only Son to take up our human nature in order to raise us up so that we could again "walk with God"; as God had intended us to do from the beginning. By taking it upon himself, Jesus Christ conquered (the culture of) death forever; so that St. Paul could say: "Death where is thy victory; where is thy sting?"

Joy, which is the fruit of love, is, therefore, the basic attitude of the Christian to life. And it is not mere human joy, still less sensual pleasure, but a participation in the very joy and ineffable bliss of God himself. This abides in the person of living faith regardless of how terrible things become here on earth. Indeed, in the depths of our soul we should not fear affliction and suffering but, like St. Rose of Lima, see it as a God-given opportunity to increase in grace and joy.

St. Rose of Lima relates as having received from the Lord himself the message that true joy is to be had only through conforming our lives to his suffering on the Cross. "Let them [us] know that the gifts of grace increase as the struggles increase. Let men take care not to stray and be deceived. This is the only true stairway to paradise and without the cross they can find no road to climb to heaven." So the saint goes on to say: "No one would complain about his cross or about troubles that might happen to him if he would come to know the scales on which they are weighed when they are distributed to men."

The face of this profound joy is visible; we have seen in it the most desperate hours of our own times in the multitude of modern martyrs, as in St. Maximilian Kolbe, dying for love of God; indeed, rejoicing in the knowledge that they are doing so.

So it is that recent popes have reminded us of the possession of joy and peace of soul even in this life through the Church despite the horrendous evils of our times. The world makes the mistake of looking for justice and peace without charity, which supposes the possession of Christian hope and faith. Thus, we have had the Apostolic Exhortation "Rejoice in the Lord" (*Gaudate in Domino*) of blessed pope Paul VI in 1975 and the present pope's "The Gospel of Joy" (*Evangelii Gaudium*) in 2013.

Dr. DeMarco's new book is a response to the same question answered by the Magisterium for our times, but from a layperson's point of view. The answer given at this level is not of course in essence different from that of the popes but complements their heartfelt exhortations. In many ways, however, the answer at this

4

level can reach many who, because of modern anti-hierarchical prejudice, even among Catholics, will not listen to the leadership of the Church.

The book is a valuable and most necessary work in directing us to the real answer to the question: "How can we cope in a world that seems to be sinking rapidly into violence and moral corruption at all levels?" Dr. DeMarco uses the same techniques and practical examples that proved so effective with his previous book. He uses analogies in the bodily and natural order of things to great effect and he brings in the testimonies of great Catholic figures, both clerical, such as Cardinal Ratzinger/Pope Benedict XVI, and lay, such as the incomparable G. K. Chesterton and the masterful Christopher Dawson, to whom our modern Catholic academics pay too little attention. Not all the major Catholic figures he quotes are of the stature of the above. But all have particular insights we can use, if in the case of some, such as Teilhard de Chardin, we would not be prepared to endorse their whole philosophy.

There are many sections of the book that bring us to recognize "those present realities," in the words of Pope Francis, that "unless effectively dealt with are capable of setting off processes of dehumanization which would then be hard to reverse." (*Evangelii Gaudium n. 51*) One of the processes that has taken a hold in a particularly virulent way in recent times is the attempt to abolish fatherhood. So insidious is this that little attempt seems to have been made even within the Catholic academic world to deal with it.

Dr. DeMarco, however, makes the restoration of what he calls the "Gift of Fatherhood" the first of the means necessary for flourishing in a fallen world. Well does he do this, and he does it very well. He perceptively notes how modern psychology is used to denigrate the natural role of the father, with Sigmund Freud a pioneer in this process. It is not without reason that St. John Paul II traces it right back to original sin. All sorts of other dehuman-

izing processes are connected with it, such as the "sexual revolution" that has succeeded spectacularly in de-moralizing present
society. If for no other reason than the splendid defense he makes
of fatherhood, Dr. DeMarco's book would rate as essential reading
for our times.

Rightly does he concentrate on virtue as the key means to effectively dealing with the grave personal and social crisis brought
upon us by "the culture of death." If I may be allowed to add
a further quote from Chesterton, written before his conversion,
when comparing the natural virtues to the purely Christian ones of
Faith, Hope and Charity, after noting the definitions of the former,
as that of justice consisting in rendering to another what is his due,
he says: "But charity means pardoning the unpardonable... Hope
means hoping when things are hopeless... And faith means be-
lieving the incredible..." (from "Paganism and Mr. Lowes Dick-
inson," Ch. 12 of Heretics by G.K. Chesterton).

Hopelessness is a true picture of the current state of the
world seen from a human point of view, and hence many have
fallen into a state of revenge, despair and loss of faith. However,
Chesterton's paradoxes bring out the great truth of things from the
divine point of view of the Christian: divine love is not against
justice; divine hope is not against human hope; divine faith is not
against reason. They simply transcend their scope and power.

What the world does not realize is that without recourse to
the supernatural help of these virtues, our natural virtues, even
that of justice, fail to protect us against, and our reason proves
impotent to remedy, the great evils that plague our existence in the
modern world. The truth is that the answer to our woes, seemingly
insuperable, lies in trust in a Saviour "who became human that we
might become divine."

Dr. DeMarco is saying no more than this. But he is able to
put it in a language that is down to earth and persuasive. There is a
great need at the present time and in the present parlous situation

of the world for more books like his.

Donald G. Boland LLB PhD

President,
Centre for Catholic Studies Inc.
Sydney, Australia

INTRODUCTION

Architects of the Culture of Death (2004), which Benjamin Wiker and I co-authored, is an analysis of the phenomenon – The Culture of Death – that the late John Paul II discussed in his encyclical, *The Gospel of Life*. The book proved successful. Ignatius Press listed it as one of its best-sellers. And it was subsequently translated into Spanish, Croatian, Estonian, Czech, and Polish. The work was an extended response to the question that the now sainted pontiff raised in that same encyclical: "How did such a situation come about?"

The extent to which the Culture of Death has been sweeping over society is alarming not only because of the facile acceptance of death that it brings, but also how much more difficult it has made it for people to choose life consistently on all its various levels. The present tension between The Culture of Death and the Culture of Life is perhaps the most critical issue of our time.

After completing my work on *Architects*, I continued to write on the subject. I was fortunate enough to place a large number of my articles in a wide variety of magazines and journals. The question concerning how a person can flourish in a fallen world became an abiding and absorbing concern for me.

How to Flourish in a Fallen World is a unified collection of some of these articles, modified to serve the purpose of the book, and organized according to three parts: "The Meaning of Morality"; "The Problem with Our Present Culture"; "The Means for Flourishing in a Fallen World." Each part incorporates 6 chapters.

It is my sincere hope that this book will assist the reader in gaining a better awareness of the present Culture of Death and a firmer resolve to work steadfastly for The Culture of Life.

Donald DeMarco is a Senior Fellow of Human Life International. He is professor emeritus at St. Jerome's University in Waterloo, Ontario, and an adjunct professor at Holy Apostles College and Seminary in Cromwell, Connecticut, and a regular columnist for St. Austin Review. Some of his recent writings may be found at Human Life International's Truth & Charity Forum.

—PART ONE—
THE MEANING OF OUR MORTALITY

THE MEANING OF LIFE

According to popular intelligence, "the meaning of life" remains an unapproachable mystery. Yet it poses a question of such fundamental importance that it cannot be ignored. The Monty Python players, in their movie, *The Meaning of Life*, did not ignore it, but turned the whole issue into a burlesque, which pleased the cynics who believe that there is no real answer to this enduring question.

The late Marlon Brando once remarked that when it comes time to take his last breath, he will say to himself, "What was that all about?" Is life just a series of disconnected and transitory events that is ultimately meaningless? Is it presumptuous even to explore whether life might hold some overriding meaning?

Philosophers have always been willing to tackle questions of fundamental human importance. Though philosophy is not exactly enjoying its heyday at the present time, philosophers continue to ponder the meaning of life. Here, it is not a question of fools rushing in where angels fear to tread, but of philosophy grasping a fundamental feature of human experience and expressing it in ordinary language.

Let us commence our pondering by drawing attention to a common greeting that transpires when two people meet each other: "How are you? How's life treating you?" Philosophically, these words imply a distinction between your being and your life. Upon further reflection, we realize that your being is in some sense prior to your life and that as soon as you begin to experience life, your being is somehow in jeopardy. Your being is like a small craft set in a stormy sea. You are, it appears, imperilled by your life.

People readily understand this, and the question, "How's life treating you?," implies that your life is distinct from your being, and that it endangers your life from the start. It also implies that you have a duty to safeguard your being that is constantly challenged by the vicissitudes of life. We express concern to each other about how we are holding up under life's continued assaults.

Here is a key to understanding the meaning of life. Its vexing purpose is most often raised when life seems to be treating us badly. In such instances, life appears to be hostile to our being, to the "I" that is subject to its apparent whims. "What meaning can life possibly have?" we ask, when it seems so contrary to our preferences. We are buffeted by life and wonder how so negative a force can have any meaning. At the same time, the deeper our experience of an absence of meaning–which is despair–the more energetically we try to find it.

It may very well be that the difficulties, trials, and challenges of life are needed for life to have meaning. René Le Senne, leader of the French "Philosophy of Spirit" school, holds that the obstacles of life have meaning because they are needed to develop human values. Virtue is often cultivated in an atmosphere of turbulence. Goethe has remarked that "Talent is nurtured in solitude; character is formed in the stormy billows of the world."

Viktor Frankl's reflections on his experience at Auschwitz, that he recorded in *Man's Search for Meaning*, is the most widely read and universally acclaimed book on the subject in the modern era. Dr. Frankl comes to the conclusion that "What man actually needs is not a tensionless state but rather the striving and struggling for some goal worthy of him." In other words, the difficulties of life are intimately bound up with its meaning. If we could take away the difficulties, our existence would become flat, flabby, and devoid of a sense of meaning.

An image from the world of nature might serve to illuminate this point. Some time ago, North Sea fishermen were surprised to discover that many of the herring they had captured died before their ship reached port. The herring were placed in vats filled with the very sea water that constituted their natural environment. But why did so many perish, and in so short a time? The fishermen finally realized that the herring had a natural enemy that, in pursuing their fleeing quarry, gave them a life stimulus needed to keep them vitalized and alive. Without this stimulus, the herring would soon perish. The fishermen then placed the enemy in the same vat with the herring. This manoeuvre, paradoxically, ensured that a far greater percentage of the herring would remain alive when the ship reached port, and therefore, fresh for market.

A tensionless or stressless life is not something we should seek. We need difficulties, obstacles, and the like, in order to mobilize us, to lift us out of the doldrums, so that we can better realize our personalities, which is to say, who we are. The meaning of life, then, is to awaken and direct the development of our personalities. In this regard, the philosophical personalism of such Catholic philosophers as Gabriel Marcel, Emmanuel Mounier, Jacques Maritain, and Pope John Paul II is most illuminating.

The lyric poet John Keats, in a famous letter he penned two years before he died, drew a distinction between a "mere intelligence" and a truly personalized "Soul." "Do you not see how necessary a World of Pains and troubles is to school an Intelligence and make it a soul?" We inhabit a world of "soul-making" where "the heart must feel and suffer in a thousand diverse ways." We know that it takes a great deal of pressure to produce a diamond. Perhaps, in a similar vein, personality is formed in an existential crucible of meaningful stress.

The character we cultivate in responding to the difficulties that life sends our way is inseparable from the formation of our distinct identities as human beings. We need the obstacles of life in order to preserve, purify, promote, and perfect our personalities. Consequently, life, including its train of disagreeable factors, has meaning because it offers us the opportunity to become authentic, fully personalized human beings. St. Ignatius of Loyola was actually expressing a great deal of love for his Jesuit priests when he prayed that they would always be persecuted. He did not form a religious community for the purpose of making his disciples comfortable, complacent, and consequently, ineffectual. We respond with courage and hope to the difficulties that life sends us and, lo and behold, discover that they have helped humanize us.

For the Zen master, "the obstacle is the path." For the Christian, the Cross is the Way.

My Telomeres Are Getting Shorter

A writer is always looking for ways in which he can express old ideas with new words. He knows that his language must be kept fresh to prevent his readers from semantic boredom, if not semantic aphasia.

In the senior circles where I spend a great deal of my social time, I hear the expression, "We're getting older," a little too often. Actually, I am weary of it. The truth is, we start getting "older" the moment our one-cell zygote replicates itself into two nearly identical cells. They are "nearly identical," I must emphasize, because, in an unmeasurably small way, our telomeres got shorter and thereby began the irreversible process of ageing which caused us to get older.

What are *telomeres*? They are the protective tips on the chromosomes of all mammals. They keep the ends of various chromosomes from accidentally becoming attached to each other. Chromosomes are the slender strands which carry the genes which are our units of inheritance, the factors that determine our physical features. Over time, as our cells continue to divide, our telomeres become progressively shorter. This takes place without the genes themselves being affected. The shorter our telomeres get, the more we are at risk for all those health problems that are associated with the ageing: cancer, arthritis, and a variety of other degenerative diseases.

Scientists tell us that when the sheep named Dolly was cloned, she began her life with telomeres that were the same age as the ewe that donated them. In other words, poor Dolly was truly old before her time. She developed obesity at a very young age and also suffered from early-onset arthritis. On Valentine's Day in the year 2002, old Dolly was euthanized.

There is rich irony in what happened to Dolly. Cloning was supposed to be a way of starting all over again. It promised to be the scientific discovery of the fountain of youth. But the ewe that provided her DNA, genes, chromosomes, and telomeres, also transmitted her age. Cloning, therefore, is not like sexual reproduction that allows new life to begin at the beginning.

Ageing, dying, getting older, is not something we can shake, though we do rage against the approaching night. We resort to bogus anti-ageing chemicals, cosmetic surgery, cryogenics, the vain hopes of transhumanism, and other desperate measures. But death remains unshakeable. Human existence is a mosaic of life and death, factors that are as tightly interwoven as telomeres are bound to their respective chromosomes.

There is a question that pundits love to ask – "How do you unscramble an egg?" The answer is, "feed it to a hen." This is not far from what C. S. Lewis had in mind when he advised, in his science fiction novel, *That Hideous Strength*, not to have dreams but to have babies. If we want to unscramble our life or achieve a sense of immortality, we must honor nature and go back to the source. Reorganization and rebirth are mysterious processes that belong to the maternal.

There is rejuvenation in the strict sense, but only by having children. It may be humbling to look at an infant and realize that he has much longer and more serviceable telomeres than we ageing on-lookers have. The cells of an infant divide at a prodigious rate, in comparison with senior citizens whose cellular activity slows to a crawl. But it also should cause us to admire the life energy that a child displays that we older folk have been steadily losing. We cannot do much about maintaining the length of our telomeres. If we want to feel rejuvenated, we should involve ourselves with children. Their spirit and energy are infectious. "The soul is healed," writes Dostoevsky, "by being with children."

A culture that approves abortion, and as it now appears, is inching toward selective infanticide, is a culture that is getting old without receiving the full benefits that children provide. To grow old, whose mandate is indelibly inscribed in our chromosomes, without any real form of rejuvenation, is to see life as a continual and irreversible experience of loss. In this context, then, growing old means that a person becomes less and less. Hence, the inevitable connection between abortion and infanticide, on the one hand, and euthanasia and assisted suicide for the elderly, on the other.

Biochemists inform us that 85-90% of cancer cells are able to divide indefinitely without their telomeres being shortened. For this reason, they can speak of cancer cells in terms of *immortality*. But their immortality is of no benefit to the human organism. In fact, their presence in the human body can be lethal. They are immortal, but not life-sustaining.

The irony here is that a little bit of death in the form of shrinking telomeres (that preclude cancer) is needed to sustain life. In a similar way, vaccination, which is the injection of a small dose of a disease, prevents the disease from overcoming the organism. So too, the difficulties that life sends our way, the "thousand natural shocks that flesh is heir to," as Hamlet says, can also serve to strengthen our life.

The function and operation of our telomeres offer us a fascinating parable. We can strengthen our own life and at the same time become rejuvenated by identifying with and working for the youngest members of the human family, even those who are threatened by abortion. In mysterious and indirect ways, we become beneficiaries of our efforts to promote and defend life.

LOVE AND HEALING

"Love and Healing" develops the theme of healing as removing that which is alien to the human being. This notion of healing is consonant with two aspects of love: affirming the self in its proper or authentic state, and restoring the wounded self to that state. Christianity owes much to the contributions of the ancient Greeks on this subject, but greatly surpasses them in its recognition of the critical importance of the body and the supreme value of love.

On June 21, 2009, Pope Benedict XVI spoke to directors, employees and patients at the *Casa Sollievo della Sofferenza* (the "Home to Relieve Suffering"). The Pontiff recalled the words of St. Padre Pio, when the hospital opened in 1956, that "the commitment of science in treating the patient [must] never be separated from a filial trust in God, infinitely tender and merciful." The saint of Pietrelcina also noted, on the hospital's first anniversary (May 5, 1957), that in the *Casa Sollievo* "the recovering, doctors, priests will be reserves of love, which, inasmuch as it abounds in one, the more it will be communicated to others."

Benedict made the comment that, "Each time one enters a

place of cure, one's thoughts turn naturally to the mystery of disease and pain, to the hope of healing and to the inestimable value
of health, which is often recognized only when it is lost."

The relationship between an atmosphere of loving care and
the process of healing brings into focus a critically important issue
that has captured the attention of philosophers, theologians, and
members of the medical profession throughout the ages. How is
it possible for love, which is essentially spiritual, to have a trans-
forming effect on the human body, which is corporeal and the natural object of scientific intervention? The answer to this timeless
question, at least in part, is related to the integral wholeness of
the human person and the natural affinity human beings have for
each other.

Love, as Pierre Teilhard de Chardin has described it, is the
"affinity between being and being." It is moreover, a radical affinity that makes possible the blending and mending of human souls.
In this sense, love is the great equalizer, having the inherent potential for being expressed between any one human being and any
other. Love, therefore, is an *affirmation* of the other, regarding the
other in his wholeness. This affirmation rests on the recognition
that a person's wholeness constitutes his original state, the state in
which he is most himself. This original state is a person's fundamental good and, as such, is a natural object of love. In the case
of people who are severely debilitated, this inner value may be
difficult to perceive. In this regard G. K. Chesterton has made the
insightful and witty comment that "It is strange that men should
see sublime inspiration in the ruins of an old church and see none
in the ruins of a man."

None of us, needless to say, exists in a state of primal wholeness. Nor is any one of us unblemished. Consequently, the second
phase of love is *restoration*. Here, love operates as the desire to
help others return, as much as is possible, to that original state of
wholeness. The simple observation of a mother bathing her child

and restoring that child to cleanliness exemplifies these two phases of love. By definition, restoration implies the original state which is the one that is affirmed. Restoration operates on a state that cannot be affirmed in itself. Love is intolerant of imperfection.

It is important to note that in most European languages, for example, the words *health, healing, wholeness*, and *holiness* are all etymologically related. Healing is a restoration of health or wholeness. We speak of "physical health" on a bodily level, "mental health" on a psychological level, "integrity," referring to the moral dimension, and "holiness," referring to spiritual wholeness.

Healing is rooted in love insofar as love desires the other to be restored to wholeness, and this restoration process presupposes the primary and primal significance of wholeness. Disease, depression, sin, and alienation are all impediments that compromise wholeness. Healing involves the removal of these impediments.

Plato regarded all impediments to wholeness as "alien" factors that do not belong to the human in which they have lodged themselves. In the third book of his *Republic,*[1] he refers to all such impediments as "evil" and specifies such evil as "an alien thing in alien souls." Evil is that which does not belong in a person and inhibits his proper functioning. Consequently, it should be removed so that the person can be truly himself again.

The process of healing for Plato, therefore, is the removal of that which is alien to a person in the interest of restoring him to wholeness. Plato's conception of personal wholeness is evident throughout his many writings. In his dialogue, *Charmides,*[2] he insists that healing must always begin in the soul. Accordingly, he writes as follows.

". . . if the head and body are to be well, you must begin by curing the soul – that is the first and essential thing: and the cure of the soul . . . has to be effected by the use of certain charms, and these charms are fair words, and by them temperance is implanted in the soul, and where temperance comes and stays, there health is speedily imparted, not only to the head, but to the whole body . . . Let no one persuade you to cure the head, until he has first given you his soul to be cured by this charm. For this . . . is the great error of our day in the treatment of human beings, [namely] that men try to be physicians of health and temperance separately."

Plato's view of healing is based on his recognition of the integral wholeness of the human being as well as the notion that the highest level subsumes the lower levels. Thus, for Plato, healing begins by curing the head. Norman Cousins, that indefatigable student of the relationship between mind and body, shows some affection for the Platonic model of healing in his 1989 book, *Head First: The Biology of Hope.*[3] He contends that "The major advances in modern science give substance to the principle that the mind of the patient creates the ambience of treatment. Belief becomes biology. The head comes first" (p. 281). Cousins is a strong advocate of psychoneuroimmunology, a new branch of medicine that explores the interaction of the brain, the endocrine system, and the immune system.

In the *Symposium,*[4] Plato's celebrated dialogue on love, the great student of Socrates and teacher of Aristotle speaks of the essential role that love plays in medicine. Referring to the expert practitioner of medicine, he writes as follows:

"Yes, gentlemen, he must be able to reconcile the jarring elements of the body, and force them, as it were, to fall in love with one another. Now, we know that the most hostile elements are the opposites — hot and cold, sweet and sour, wet and dry, and so on — and if, as I do myself, we are to believe these poets of ours, it was his skill in imposing love and concord upon these opposites that enabled our illustrious progenitor Asclepius to found the science of medicine.

"And so, gentlemen, I maintain that medicine is under the sole direction of the god of love . . . ."

Plato's reference to Asclepius, the god of medicine, is significant. Just before he died, Socrates remembered a debt. "I owe a cock to Asclepius," he said to Crito. "Will you remember to pay the debt?"[5] These were the last words Socrates was to utter. The father of moral philosophy was referring to the Greek custom of propitiating the god of medicine following medical treatment. The cock is a poor man's offering. It is believed that it was made on behalf of Plato who, being ill, was unable to be with his dearest friend when Socrates drew his final breath.

In Plato's hierarchic vision, the physician stands in the middle between the body which he endeavours to heal and an ideal which he seeks to imitate. The mind can heal the body because knowledge of sickness does not itself confer sickness. At the same time, the mind needs an ideal so that it can resist being infected in such a way that evil becomes a property of the soul. Plato, of course, knew nothing of the immune system or bacterial infections. His view of medicine seems, to the modern physician, unacceptably idealistic. Nonetheless, Plato made important contributions to the love/healing discussion and even today, physicians are referred to, in certain quarters, as Aesculapians.

According to Greek polytheism, Asclepius was just one of many gods. Hence, the love and healing that he represented was not universal among the gods. By contrast, Christianity is monotheistic and the love that is attributed to God is thoroughly divine. In fact, for Christians, God is identified as "Love." Jesus, the Son of God gave central importance to love and healing during his brief ministry on earth. Of the 3,779 verses in the four Gospels, 727, or nearly one/fifth, are related specifically to the healing of physical and mental illnesses and the resurrection of the dead. In most cases, Jesus combined the speaking of words with touching. His practice of touching began a tradition which survives to the present of the "laying on of hands." In three instances Jesus uses saliva in exercising his healing. Nor was his healing ministry constrained by social conventions. At least six of his healings took place on the Sabbath.

Plato philosophised about healing. Jesus put it into practice. With the rise of Christianity, many Aesculapian shrines were transformed into Christian Churches. Writing about the great transition from the Greek to the Christian view of love and healing, J. W. Provonsha, MD, makes the following observation:

"It has become traditional to identify modern doctors with a long line of historic greats reaching back to the impressive Hippocrates... But sometimes it is forgotten that medicine owes its greatest debt not to Hippocrates, but to Jesus. It was this humble Galilean who more than any other figure in history bequeathed to the healing arts their essential meaning and spirit... Physicians would do well to remind themselves that without His spirit, medicine degenerates into depersonalized methodology, and its ethical code becomes a mere legal system. Jesus brings to methods and codes the corrective of love without which true healing is rarely possible. The spiritual 'Father of Medicine' was not Hippocrates of the Island of Cos, but Jesus of the town of Nazareth."[6]

Nonetheless, something of the philosophy of the ancient Greeks survives. Morton T. Kelsey states in his book, *Healing and Christianity*, and writing from a Christian perspective, that "As this Spirit resides in us we build up defenses against alien forces so that they cannot so easily attack and possess us."[7] Kelsey goes on to say that "Love is an invitation to God's Spirit" which serves to protect us from "alien domination."[8] He sees Christ's command to love one another as more than an ethical maxim. It also carries profound healing implications.

Kelsey may have been echoing the thought of St. Augustine who, in one of his sermons[9] wrote: "When... Christ first preached to the few who believed, he was mocked by multitudes. Nevertheless by the power of the cross, the blind saw, the lame walked, the lepers were cleansed so that all might come to know, that even among the powers of this world, there is nothing more powerful than the humility of God."[10]

The Christian approach to love and healing accepts the fundamental importance of the wholeness of the person and that evil is something alien. In this regard, it owes much to Ancient Greece. But it goes far beyond these ancients roots in that it holds love to be unequivocally divine, expresses love in a more personal manner, and understands the appropriateness of ministering directly to the body.

Plato, idealist that he was, failed to appreciate the supreme importance of the body. Modern research on the therapeutic value of touching would have been an eye-opener for him. The healing power of touch is so natural to human beings that it can be observed among premature babies. The University of Massachusetts Memorial, for example, has co-bedded at least 100 sets of multiple birth preemies. Observing the practice over a period of five years, the hospital staff there has not found a single case of twin-to-twin infection. In addition, clinical studies have shown that premature twins enjoy substantial benefits when they are placed in the same bed together. Researchers Gayle Kasparian and Mary Whalen, report the following benefits:

- Decreased number of sleep apnea problems.
- Improved blood-oxygen levels.
- Increased weight gain.
- Better feeding.
- Greater temperature regulation.
- Decreased agitation.
- Decreased length of hospital stays and likelihood of re-admission.[11]

Someone has said that we need four hugs a day for survival, eight for maintenance, and twelve for growth. This may not be entirely accurate, but it does illuminate an important truth about human beings: "We touch therefore we are" is incomparably more revealing of the nature of human beings than "I think therefore I am."

Plato, though not to his discredit, knew nothing of the immune system. Had he become acquainted with this natural marvel, he would undoubtedly have radically altered his views on healing and fully accepted the importance of the corporeal.

Of all the mysteries of modern science, the immune system's capacity for distinguishing between the *self* and the *non-self* must rank at or near the top.[12] In order to protect itself against foreign substances, the immune system generates 100 billion (1011) different kinds of immunological receptors. No matter what the shape or form of the enemy invader, there will be some correlative receptor to recognize it and effect its elimination.

"Self," in this context, refers to the person solely on a physiological level and does not include, *per se*, the psychological, moral, and spiritual dimensions of the human person. The "non-self," therefore, is also understood on this same physiological plane. At the same time, the human person is a moral, spiritual, psychosomatic unity, and what transpires on one level may have an effect on another. Although the human person is, indeed, an organic entity, it is possible to distinguish these different levels.

Added to the mystery of how the immune system distinguishes self from non-self is its ability to recognize foreign carbohydrates, nucleic acids, and proteins amidst those which exist within the organism that are exceedingly similar to them in structure and shape. When the immune system is functioning properly, it never gets activated by self substances and unerringly responds to those that belong to the non-self. When it is not functioning properly, the distinction between self and non-self is blurred and diseases of autoimmunity occur.

The functioning of the healthy immune system in protecting the self against the non-self serves as a prototype of the binary manner in which higher levels of the integrated person operate. For example, on a psychological level, hope is consonant with the overall health of the self; despair acts as something alien to that good, and consequently as self-destructive. Karl Menninger, psychiatrist and co-founder of the Menninger Foundation in Topeka, Kansas, views "hope" as one of the "sublime expressions of the life instinct." Norman Cousins speaks of hope as a "powerful prescription." [13]

The immune system, by nature, is not relativistic. It firmly values the self and just as firmly disvalues threats to the self. It sees no middle ground. Needless to say, the immune system operates below the plane of consciousness. But it is both a prototype and model for all the higher levels of the self.

The self on a moral level relates to the person's "authenticity" and is related to freedom. This is a favourite theme among a myriad of existential personalists from Kierkegaard to Karol Wojtyla. It is possible for a person to choose to be estranged from himself. In trying to be what he is not, he allows a "non-self" to displace his authentic self. We know that pride precedes a fall. Because pride is the temptation to be what one is not, it is potentially ruinous of one's authentic personality. On the other hand, through conscious effort, one can freely choose humility which casts out pride and restores the authentic self. The proud person is inclined to insist, for example, that a particular wrong idea is right simply because it is in his head. He tends to lose his ability to make the more important judgment that the idea does not *belong* there. He no longer sees the alien idea as part of the non-self. In other words, a proud person tries to become something other than who he truly is. His egoism fails to dispel the ideas that do not truly belong to him. A more humble individual will be less inclined to believe that being in one's head is all that is required to validate an idea. He wants his ideas to conform to truth. He knows that such truthful ideas belong to him as part of his authentic self. Humility is consonant with his real identity.

In considering another of the Deadly Sins, lust, we find the same transition from self to non-self taking place. A person who is driven by lust may welcome this potentially ruinous disposition because it is convenient or because it promises pleasure. But lust fractures the personality, allowing one part to dominate or even displace the whole. Temperance, on the other hand, is the moral virtue that holds the self together. It ensures that various desires and inclinations are brought into harmony with each other. It honors the value of human wholeness.

On a philosophical level, truth safeguards the self and allows its development, while persistence in error can have a disintegrating effect. On a spiritual level, the binary opposites involve being and nothingness, theism and atheism.

We may envision the immune system as the base of a pyramid. This is the broad base of the physiological level that affirms the self and opposes the non-self. Above that we find the psychological level that accepts hope and rejects despair, the moral level that welcomes goodness and eschews evil, the philosophical level that embraces truth and shuns error, and finally, at the apex of the pyramid, the spiritual level that unites with God and avoids the abyss of nothingness.

Healing is needed on all these five levels of the person if he is to attain maximum wholeness. Moreover, these different levels can, as Plato noted, have beneficent effects on the lower levels. World famous immunologist, Depak Chopra, has shown that even looking at a picture of Mother Teresa can strengthen the immune system by producing additional T cells. Viktor Frankl, founder of logotherapy, has written about a condition he refers to as "noögenic neurosis," [14] a psychological disorder that is caused by alien ideas. Norman Cousins and his medical associates have reported instances where patients, once they were freed from depression and despair, showed an increase in the number of cancer-fighting immune cells.

Because the human person is essentially one being and not a multitude of conflicting factors, it is not surprising that healing on one level can have salutary effects on other levels. It is equally true that a disharmonious condition on one level can have a deleterious effect on other levels.

Love embraces the whole person. This presents an additional reason for the physician to concern himself with all the various levels of the patient's personhood. For good work in one area can be quickly undone because of neglect in other areas. The old adage of a sound mind in a sound body should not be viewed in a dualistic fashion. Rather, we should see the soundness of mind and the soundness of body as aspects of the same integrated person.

In his *Summa Theologica* St. Thomas Aquinas responds to the question whether pain and sorrow can be mitigated by the compassion of friends (*"Utrum dolor et tristitia mitigentur per compassionem amicorum?*).[15] He gives two reasons to support his affirmative answer. The first reason is that sorrow has a depressing effect, like weight from which we try to unburden ourselves, so that when a man sees others saddened by his own sorrow, it seems as though others are bearing the burden with him, striving, as it were, to lessen the weight. In this way, the burden of sorrow becomes lighter. The next reason, which Aquinas regards as the better one, is because of the pleasure he receives when he experiences the love of his friends, since every pleasure assuages sorrow.

Aquinas' response is based on his underlying conviction that love has the capacity for positive, healing transformations. This understanding of love is rooted in the "being-to-being" affinity that exists between human beings. Aquinas amplifies this point in another passage of his *Summa*[16] where he states that "another's actions, if they are good, are reckoned as one's own good, by reason of the power of love, which makes a man to regard his friend as one with himself." Love unifies, and in this unifying process, heals. Even the transition from loneliness to community is a form of healing.

Every human being has a healing potential. If love does not provide a healing cure, in certain instances, it nonetheless can relieve suffering. The ideal of *Casa Sollievo della Sofferenza* should be shared by all: physicians and patients, priests and parishioners, saints and sinners, parents and children, neighbours and strangers.

THE FRAGILE DEW-DROP

We live, scientists tell us, in a four-dimensional space-time continuum. In a way that is difficult to grasp, space and time are profoundly inter-related. But the imagination lives in a fifth dimension—Dimension H—the realm of the hypothetical. *What is* and *what could be* lie in tantalizingly close proximity to each other, separated only by our free choices. Free choice is the dramatic switch that separates *what will be* from *what could be*. Nothing is more important in life than choosing rightly.

These thoughts came to mind recently while I watched one of my very favorite movies, *Carnegie Hall* (1947). I was in awe as I observed and listened to that pianistic titan, Arthur Rubinstein, as he performed Chopin's heroic A-flat *Polonaise* and Manuel de Falla's demonic "Ritual Fire Dance." Strength and subtlety, power and passion! Rubinstein always appeared to me as indomitable. Yet, the imagination knows otherwise. Dimension H led to a radically different outcome.

I picked up his autobiography — *Arthur Rubinstein: My Young Years* (Knopf, 1973) — and re-read its opening words: "My life was saved by my Aunt Salomea. A seventh child eight years after the last-born, I was utterly unwanted by my parents, and if it hadn't been for the enthusiastic persuasion of aunt Salomea Meyer, my intrusion into this valley of suffering might have been prevented."

Rubinstein's life could have been snuffed out as easily as I could have turned off the TV. "I rang the bell at the gate of life," the great pianist tells us, "as a belated and rather unwanted guest."

Life, as the poet John Keats describes it, is "A fragile dew-drop on its perilous way from a tree's summit" (*Sleep and Poetry*). Life begins in the embrace of love, truly a lofty beginning. But then, the perilous journey is in the care of capricious choice. Or, in the case of the adult Rubinstein, the supporting power of a belt from a worn-out robe.

Rubinstein was penniless, hungry, and depressed. His career was not unfolding as he had hoped. Suicide beckoned to him. But the belt he used to hang himself tore apart, and the man who was destined to become the 20th Century's most romantic concert pianist, fell to the floor with a crash. Half-conscious, he dragged himself to his piano and cried himself out in music. Then, out of a chaos of thought, came a blazing revelation. At that moment, he tells us, he "discovered the secret of happiness," one that he continued to cherish throughout his life: "Love life for better or for worse, without conditions" (p. 255).

Being a traveler along the paths of Dimension H, I then imagined changing the channel, once *Carnegie Hall* had concluded, to watch *The Farmer's Daughter* (also 1947). This is the motion picture that won an Academy Award for its star, Loretta Young. But there was no such movie because Loretta Young never existed.

Miss Young's mother, at age 23, was raising her two daughters. When she became pregnant with her third child, her younger daughter was just nine months old. Both her husband, for financial reasons, and her doctor, for medical reasons, advised her to undergo an abortion. It seemed to be the sensible thing to do. After much confusion and an ocean of tears, she sought the assistance of Father Ildefonsa, the priest who had instructed her in her faith.

She decided to have the baby and named her eight-pound girl, Loretta. The young mother's health improved and, well into her eighties, was recognized as one of the foremost interior decorators in California.

Years later, Loretta, now married and 2½ months pregnant with her second child, found herself in a situation similar to the one her mother had experienced. Her Hollywood studio strongly advised her to abort or forfeit a prospective $4.5 million contract. When she refused to comply, the studio criticized her for being more interested in having a family than having a career in motion pictures.

Loretta had her baby and lost her contract. But the following year she won an Oscar for her role in *The Farmer's Daughter*. Her former studio, realizing that she had become a great box office attraction, then offered her an even more lucrative contract. Her rejection was, as she puts it, one of the most satisfying "No's" of her life.

My imagination returned to the highway of Dimension H. This time, it was January of 2009. I turned the TV channel to ABC to see if super-athlete Tim Tebow could lead his Florida "Gators" to an NCAA championship against the vaunted Oklahoma "Sooners" who, at that time were ranked #1 in the nation.

Tebow was a legend even as a high school athlete. He was listed among the top 33 high school football players in the state of Florida's 100 year history. His high school stats were truly mind-boggling: 9,810 passing yards, 3,186 rushing yards, 95 touchdowns passing, and 62 touchdowns rushing. One of the highlights of his high school career was finishing a game on a broken leg.

In college, as an All-American quarterback, he was the first college football player to *rush* and *pass* for 20 or more touchdowns in a single season. He became the first sophomore to win the Heisman Trophy, an award emblematic of being the year's most outstanding college football player. Tebow's leadership qualities and his determination to win were unsurpassed. Could he carry the "Gators" to an NCAA championship.

But neither Mr. Tebow nor any of his teammates could be found anywhere on TV. What had happened? Had his fragile dewdrop of life been prematurely extinguished?

Bob and Pam Tebow were Christian missionaries in the Philippines. While pregnant with Tim, Pam contracted amoebic dysentery through contaminated drinking water. Her doctor informed her that the medications she needed to recover would result in irreversible damage to the child she was carrying. He also warned that continuing her pregnancy would endanger her life. Therefore, her doctor advised an abortion.

Tim was born in 1987, robust and healthy. His mother survived the delivery very nicely. Today, Tim Tebow stands six-foot-three and weighs 235 pounds. He is an elusive runner, accurate passer, and very difficult to bring down. He has also joined his parents in their missionary activities.

Shifting from the realm of the imagination back to reality, I witnessed, with much pleasure, the Tebow-led "Gators" defeat the Oklahoma "Sooners" 24-14, and lay claim to the National Championship.

Charles Dickens' *Christmas Carol* and Frank Capra's *It's A Wonderful Life* are very successful ventures into Dimension H. The former tells of the grim tragedies that would unfold unless the heart of Ebenezer Scrooge underwent a thawing. The latter tells of the terrible void that would have been created if George Bailey never lived.

A pianist, an actress, and an athlete, all pre-eminent in their respective fields, survived the threat of abortion and brought to the world stage superlative images of beauty, grace, and strength. The mandate to "choose life" thus becomes more compelling and more eloquent when we consider how much the world would have lost had this trio been prematurely extinguished, as well as the joys of life which they, themselves, would never have experienced.

The superhighway of Dimension H, though purely imaginary, can be of great service in recapturing the limitless potential of life and the sheer emptiness of its opposite. It behoves us, therefore, to choose life.

THE FALL OF ICONS

A writer who practices his art at home does not want to turn his place of residence into a library warehouse. And so, every so often, in order to maintain a dynamic equilibrium between acquisitions and dispersals, he must sift through his material and separate the transitory from the enduring. It is a practice akin to gardening in which one separates the weeds from the perennials. Some material remains stubbornly attached to time, while other material becomes the stuff of history. Or so one believes. It is not an exact science.

I was engaged in such sifting recently and enjoyed the serendipitous feeling of discovering literary items that seemed to improve with time. One item, however, arrested my attention in a jarring manner. It was the cover feature for the July 17, 1989 issue of *Time*: "Death By Gun: America's Toll in One Typical Week." Why would I hold onto this issue for more than two decades? I surmise that it was to remind me of the many mature souls who die violently before their time, their lives coming to an end in great numbers, like falling leaves. The words "before their time," convey a piercing sadness: what could be, will not be. There can be no turning back.

Time dedicated a 28-page portfolio in this issue to memorialize the deaths of 464 Americans who were killed by gunfire over the course of a single week. In order to further humanize this harrowing statistic, it provided the faces of most of these casualties. Re-visiting this issue is like walking through a cemetery, but even more poignant because one knows that all these deaths were unnecessary. Each face evoked a shudder. The old Roman, Terence, was right: "I am man, I consider nothing human alien to me" (*Homo sum, humani nihil a me alienum puto*). It is the nature of any genuine pro-life sensibility to be moved by the death of anyone.

The more I studied the specific causes of these deaths, however, the more I realized that these tragedies were not so much the result of guns, but from a loss of the will to live and the inability of people to get along with each other. A large proportion of the deaths were by suicide. How many suicides took place that week, I wondered, in which the gun was not the instrument of death? The real enemy of life lurked deeper than the gun.

On page 18 I saw a face that I recognized. It belonged to Thomas Stallcup who, at age 67, turned a shotgun on himself. In his heyday he played shortstop for the Cincinnati Reds under the name Virgil Stallcup (what a great name!). I was once the proud owner of his baseball card. He was No. 108 in the 1951 *Playball* series. His portrait displayed the epitome of joy and confidence. The fact that his career stats were indeed modest (his lifetime batting average is .241) did not matter. To young baseball card collectors, he was an icon, a success story, a hero larger than life. And now, *Time* informs me, this erstwhile role model is now a grim statistic who has been absorbed by an even grimmer statistic – 464. The fact that the photo that *Time* selected was the same one that appeared on his card, made the pictorial announcement of his death morbidly ironic. Icons are not supposed to fall!

Hollywood stars are also regarded as larger than life, though the disparity between their image and their behavior is the embarrassing grist for tabloid journalism. We believed in Virgil Stallcup, we youthful, naïve baseball card collectors. It is shocking to learn that there came a time in his life when he may not have believed in himself.

Life, as the poet John Keats describes it, is "A fragile dewdrop on its perilous way from a tree's summit" (*Sleep and Poetry*). The great paradox is that our greatest value, life, travels with fragility as its constant companion. Hence, the profound poignancy of human existence. "We are all in the same boat in a stormy sea," wrote G. K. Chesterton, "and we owe each other a terrible loyalty."

Why, we may ask, does society view those who try to prevent suicide as humanitarians, and those who try to prevent abortion as fanatics? Both these cohorts are defending life. No "seamless garment" here. It is fair to conclude that our society is ambivalent about life. The fragility can be fearful, and the storms can be startling. And that's the core of the problem. Life demands courage, support, faith, and hope. It does not arrive without its challenges. And who amongst us can meet these challenges alone?

We have detached "choice" from community and are now paying a heavy price on a community level. We have been duped by the myth of autonomy. Yet, not even Major League baseball players are autonomous, though they may appear to be when looking invincible on their bubblegum cards. None of us is larger than life. Nonetheless, each of us is larger than being a mere individual. We are communal beings called to love each other. That's not how we get ourselves on baseball cards, but that may be the best way to avoid being part of the kind of grim statistic that *Time* assembled more than two decades ago.

THE IMPORTANCE OF THE FUNERAL MASS

The Funeral Mass is our ultimate declaration of hope for a soul's passage into eternal life, that is, into Purgatory or beyond. It is often accompanied by tears, but it is essentially a joyful occasion, for the hope is solemnly and prayerfully expressed that another soul will ultimately enter the kingdom of heaven. "The world is only peopled," as St. Francis de Sales once wrote, "to people heaven."

I attended, recently, what most, if not all the people present regarded as a joyful Funeral Mass. It took place in a small Polish parish where the church and its adjacent elementary school and cemetery form the spiritual center of parish life. The proximity of these concrete images of life, death, and resurrection provide parishioners with an unmistakable down-to-earth realism.

The deceased passed away just shy of his 88th birthday. In one sense, he was a simple man who earned his bread by cleaning hallway floors in various institutions. More significantly, he was lighting corridors through which his children and grandchildren would pass to discover more enterprising endeavors. The pathfinder is no less important than those who benefit from the path he blazes. Death, of course, is the great leveler, making equal the high and the low, the rich and the poor, the celebrated and the hidden. How we live in the eyes of God, needless to say, is the only thing that really counts.

But the lowly in the eyes of the world can be capable of extraordinary virtue. It was said of the deceased that he never had a bad word to say about anyone. Appropriately, the following words of St. Faustyna were inscribed on his obituary card:

> Help me, O Lord, that my tongue
> may be merciful, so that I should
> never speak negatively of my
> neighbor, but have a word of
> comfort and forgiveness for all.

He once lost a chess game to his brother, an event that proved very disappointing to his daughter. Though a man of few words, he had an important lesson he wanted to give her. "There is no dishonor in losing to a worthy opponent," he said. Then, so that his daughter would not regard him as a "loser," he added: "If one can rejoice over his brother's victory, he cannot be said to be a loser." Here is some wisdom that could be most beneficial, especially, these days, to sports celebrities.

While he served in World War II he always felt that he was under God's special protection. At one time, he came perilously close to death. A Russian soldier was about to assassinate him when fate (or Providence) intervened. At the very last second, the Russian was dispatched by another soldier. I looked at two of his darling little grand-daughters with new appreciation, realizing how close they came to never being. We are all beneficiaries of Divine Providence, much more than we can possibly realize.

Abundantly evident at the Funeral Mass was the love of the family, the faith of the community, and the loyalty of friends. Afterwards, there was the festivity of good food and sparkling fellowship. The experience altogether was, indeed, joyful, though there was a note of expressed sadness.

At the close of the Mass, the celebrant commented on how sad it is that Funeral Masses are becoming less common. Why is it that even Catholics seem less enthused about eternal life? Is this symptomatic of a general anti-life attitude that has infected what that great Polish Pontiff, Blessed John Paul II called, "The Culture of Death"?

I thought of the contrast between the Funeral Mass which emphasizes Life after Death, and the Shopping Mall, which I find to be a form of Death after Life. The contrast is far from frivolous.

People come to the Shopping Mall with their desire for things: clothes, furnishings, trinkets, gadgets. Many of these things are not meant to last for longer than a season. Being passé can be more deadly than merely passing on. In time, after their brief period of usefulness, these things pass through various stages of death. They become out-of-fashion, clutter, grist for the garage sale, and finally reach their nadir of value when classified by that dishonorable term, "junk." And then it is time, not for the cemetery, but for the junkyard.

The American essayist Maclin Horton has, I believe, put things in the proper perspective when he writes: "The mall is a place of death in life, and therefore it is appropriate to be sad there; the cemetery is a place of life in death, a place in which to rejoice and be glad."

Merchandise purchased at the Shopping Mall depreciates as soon as it is possessed by the consumer. The rewards for a soul who lives a life of virtue, as Christ has promised, is a hundredfold. When our own day arrives, we could all benefit from a Funeral Mass which could very well give us the extra boost we need in order to get into heaven.

—PART TWO—
THE PROBLEM WITH OUR
PRESENT CULTURE

CULTURE VS. CIVILIZATION

At the outset of his diatribe against religion, *The Future of an Illusion*, Sigmund Freud makes the sweeping pronouncement, "I scorn to distinguish between culture and civilization." This pronouncement reveals the heart of Freud's philosophy of culture. The father of psychoanalysis does not look favorably upon the possible transition of culture to civilization since, as he contends, "every individual is virtually an enemy of civilization." For Freud, civilization places too many restrictions on man's need for instinctive satisfactions and too many obstacles in his path toward happiness. In this sense, civilization is his enemy. It is precisely because Freud stood in opposition to any cultural aspirations to higher modes of civilization, that Philip Rieff, editor of the ten-volume *Collected Papers of Sigmund Freud*, referred to him as "the champion of the second best."

The objective of this essay is to present the Catholic view that just as the individual person aspires to better things, so too, does culture (which is a society of persons) aspire to higher modes of civilization. Civilization is the crown of culture. Religion is necessary in order to effect this transition, as it has been throughout the centuries. Pope Benedict XVI, in *Truth and Tolerance*, makes the comment that, "In all known historical cultures, religion is an essential element of culture, is indeed its determinative center; it is religion that determines the scale of values and, thereby, the inner cohesion and hierarchy of all these cultures." Moral growth cannot take place unless it thrives in the presence of something higher. But it is equally important to introduce the notion of truth in order to distinguish religion from superstition.

Religion, truth, and *culture,* then, constitute three pillars of civilization. Religion reminds people that they have a destiny that transcends their momentary satisfactions. Truth helps to insure that religion is guiding them along a realistic path. Culture is the irremovable matrix in which man first plants his feet and begins to hope for something better.

Catholicism is most assuredly not a "champion of the second best." And this is precisely why it meets with no end of criticism and complaint. For it urges human beings to endure great difficulties and continuing struggles in order to realize more fully their humanity and their reflections as creatures made in the image of God. Life is taxing, but it can also be purifying.

Culture is omnipresent and irremovable. Whereas people might question the reality of God or the discoverability of truth, no one can doubt the persistent and unmistakable presence of culture. Because of this fact, there is a tendency inherent in culture to exclude religion and truth so that culture can become self-sufficient. This is a process known as *enculturation* or *acculturation.* Various attempts throughout history to exclude religion and truth, however, have failed. They have failed primarily because they deny the ineradicable need in the human being for God and the truth about himself that is indispensable for justice, peace, and mutual cooperation.

Pontius Pilate famously set truth aside and in so doing, invited the frenzy of the mob. We observe in today's world how relativism attempts to displace truth, but not to open the door for tolerance, but for something that Pope Benedict XVI has aptly labeled, "the dictatorship of relativism." In the absence of truth, either the mob or the dictator prevails.

The rejection of religion is made in the interest of making culture purely secular. This strategy has been advanced, strangely enough, even by Christian theologians. William O. Fennell, for example, in his "Theology of True Secularity," maintains that God created a secular world and populated it with autonomous men free to use it. Fennell then argues that, "in Jesus Christ, God has rescued the world from man's 'religiousness' and restored it to its original 'secularity,' and in him has given back to man the freedom which he lost when he sought to make his culture a religious and therefore an idolatrous thing."

The fact that Christian theologians, no less, and there are many of them, have viewed the function of religion as something that should be eradicated in order to prepare the way for secularization is a good indication of the seductive power culture has to tempt people to reject anything that is not an image of itself. Religion, needless to say, is not "idolatrous" if it coincides with truth. As an ally of truth, and therefore science, it becomes a requisite factor in the advancement of civilization.

Marcus Tullius Cicero, in the year 44 B.C., advised that, "we should do ourselves and our countrymen a great deal of good, if we were to root superstition out entirely." The great Roman statesman was pleading for the abolition of superstition, but for the retention of religion. We do not need superstition, he proposed, but we do need religion. For those who had trouble seeing any difference between the two, Cicero provided a distinguishing factor, their relationship with science: "That there is some eternal Being who stands out above the rest, and that the human race ought to serve and admire Him, is an admission that the beauty of the universe and the orderliness of the celestial bodies compels us to make. Therefore, just as religion, being associated with natural science, ought actually to be propagated, so every root of superstition ought to be weeded out (*On Divination*, 148-9)."

Cicero's clear grasp of the consonance between religion and reason is worthy of inclusion in John Paul II's longest encyclical, *Fides et Ratio* (Faith and Reason). The Church loves reason because it loves truth. And one important reason for loving truth is that She loves freedom.

Jacques Maritain opens his study on *The Things That Are Not Caesar's* with the following impassioned statement concerning the distinction between the spiritual and the temporal powers:

> Nothing is more important for the freedom of souls and the good of mankind than properly to distinguish between these two powers: nothing in the language of the day, has so great a *cultural* value. It is common knowledge that the distinction is the achievement of the Christian centuries and their glory.

Failure to make this distinction opens the way to reducing the human being to the level of a pawn of the state, enclosed within a narrow secular framework. Recognizing and affirming man's higher destiny allows him to exercise his God-given freedom as a person and to enjoy those spiritual realities that are not contained within the confining realm of Caesar. The purely secular view absorbs the spiritual into the temporal and denies man his inalienable right to be who he is, namely, a being who has a spiritual dimension and an innate capacity to know truth and utilize his freedom. Freud's final sentence in his *Future of An Illusion* is a lucid and disturbing example of his view of man despiritualized: "No, our science is no illusion. But an illusion it would be to suppose that what science cannot give us we can get elsewhere."

The truth of man — the anthropological realism that is the centerpiece of John Paul II's personalism — provides him with the real possibility of working effectively within his culture in order to bring about greater realizations of civilization. Just as the acting person has a civilizing effect on culture, so too, does civilization have a civilizing effect on the person.

The ultimate purpose of culture, then, beyond cultivating the more superficial differences of language, lifestyle, cuisine, forms of celebration, and so on, is to contribute to the development of personality in the process of establishing a civilization. As we fail to effect the proper interplay of culture, religion, and truth, we become absorbed in and enslaved by culture, and lose sight of who we are and where we are going.

The Catholic view of civilization is, in its basic outline, as sound as it is simple. Furthermore, it is also as revolutionary as it is realistic. Nonetheless, the attractions of the *status quo*, inclining people toward an almost exclusive preoccupation with making a living and keeping up with the Joneses, has been an important factor in bringing about a certain lack of appreciation, or even awareness, of what is needed in order to maintain a civilization.

The distinguished Catholic historian, Christopher Dawson, has recorded the following observation in his book, *The Crisis of Western Education*:

> Our modern Western secularized culture is a kind of hothouse growth. On the one hand, man is sheltered from the direct impact of reality, while on the other he is subjected to a growing pressure which makes for social conformity. He seldom has to think for himself or make vital decisions. His whole life is spent inside highly organized artificial units — factory, trade union, office, civil service, party — and his success or failure depends on his relations with this organization.

In a similar vein, though in a more psychological than sociological sense, Ernest Becker states, in his Pulitzer Prize winning

book, *The Denial of Death*: "When one lives in the liberation atmosphere of Berkeley, California, or in the intoxications of small
doses of unconstriction in a therapeutic group in one's home town,
one is living in a hothouse atmosphere that shuts out the reality of
the rest of the planet, the way things really are in the world."

Pope Benedict XVI is particularly aggrieved when he ob-
serves the European landscape. In *Without Roots* (2006), which he
co-authored with Marcello Pera, the Holy Father makes the diagnosis that "Europe seems hollow, as if it were internally paralyzed
by a failure of its circulatory system that is endangering its life."
Specifically, he enumerates three phenomena that are contributing to this necrosis. The first is a widespread disregard for human
rights and human dignity. In the concrete sphere of biology, in
reference to cloning, the freezing and storing of human fetuses
for research purposes and for organ transplants, stem-cell research
where human embryos are deliberately destroyed, one finds clear
evidence that the notion of rights and dignity do not apply to the
human unborn.

The second factor relates to the undermining of monogamous marriage through easier forms of divorce, widespread co-
habitation, and the popular acceptance of a hedonistic lifestyle.
Paradoxically, as monogamous marriage is being undermined,
there is a clamor for homosexual "marriage." If same-sex unions
are perceived to have the same moral standing as monogamous,
heterosexual marriages, the Pontiff concludes, "then we are truly
facing a dissolution of the image of humankind bearing consequences that can only be extremely grave."

The third factor pertains to the decline of religion, particularly the practice of Christianity. To a significant extent, a loss of
a sense of the sacred has been replaced by multiculturalism. Yet it
is a spurious form of multiculturalism that routinely tolerates acts
that dishonor Christianity in the name of freedom of speech. Such
tolerance is not extended to other religions. Pope Benedict does

not believe that a true multiculturalism can survive without a genuine respect for the sacred. Speaking for Christianity, he reminds us that, "it is our duty to cultivate within ourselves respect for the sacred and to show the face of the revealed God, of the God who has compassion for the poor and the weak, for widows and orphans, for the foreigner; the God who is so human that He Himself became man, a man who suffered, and who by His suffering with us gave dignity and hope to our pain."

Of the three factors that the Pope enumerates, the first two pertain to truth: the truth of man, including his dignity and rights; the truth of marriage in its traditional, universal and Biblical sense as the union of a man and a woman. The third factor pertains to religion.

Pope Benedict, therefore, is urging Europe to embrace the pillars of truth and religion so that it can overcome its culture of "self-hatred" and be restored to health.

Marcello Pera, though an unbeliever, is in agreement with Benedict's assessment to a remarkable degree while averring that, "Christianity has been the greatest force in Western history." He deplores the current relativism that is sweeping Europe, contending that it has "debilitated our Christian defenses and prepared us for surrender." He fully agrees with Benedict's diagnosis that Europe has "lost the capacity for self-love." In fact, as he adds, the situation is "nothing short of pathological." "How," says Pera in a tone of near desperation, "can we restore realism to Europe?"

Christopher Dawson offers us an image of hope when he tells Christians that they can contribute to the revitalization of civilization if they would only assume their appropriate roles as Christians. Though the following message was penned in 1952, it has a fresh and timely quality that is perfectly harmonious with the current mind and expressed hopes of Benedict XVI:

However secularized our modern civilization may become, this sacred tradition [Christianity] remains like a river in the desert, and a genuine religious education can still use it to irrigate the thirsty lands and to change the face of the world with the promise of new life. The great obstacle is the failure of Christians themselves to understand the depth of that tradition and the inexhaustible possibilities of new life that it contains (*Understanding Europe*).

Culture, religion, and truth are three *pillars* of civilization. The image of the pillar denotes firmness, strength, and support. At the same time, however, it is imperfect. The three pillars of culture, religion, and truth are not discrete entities that can be separated from one another. They, in fact, interpenetrate, intertwine, flow into each other. Civilization depends entirely on the proper interweaving of these three factors.

If culture is the soil, truth is the light, and religion is the sun. The growth that is the movement from culture to civilization requires the blended and coordinated activities of all three of these dynamic forces.

Scholars of antiquity have alleged that if the great and broad contributions of the ancient Greeks could be distilled into a single word, that word would be *aspiration*. All human beings experience dissatisfaction and discontent with their lot. They naturally desire a better state. Therefore, they have a natural desire to advance from culture in the broad sense to civilization, or what Christopher Dawson has termed, "super-culture." Religion makes this advance possible; truth makes it practicable. Though human beings have the option to suppress their aspirations and settle for "second best," the Catholic view urges them to live in loving relationships with their neighbors and work together for a better tomorrow. For the Greeks, "aspiration" is a description of the soul; for Catholics, it also includes the supernaturally infused virtue of hope. Christ provides the objective correlative for our aspirations. Catholics have little excuse for avoiding their role in helping to shape culture into a civilization.

The Godless World around Us

The most common objection to God's existence is the presence of human suffering. How can there be a God when there is so much suffering in the world? This searing question is reiterated endlessly.

I have always sensed that behind this question is the presumption that if the questioner himself were God, he would have created a world in which human beings would never suffer. The assumption is truly stupendous because it suggests, to supply words to the one asking the question – "If I were God, I would do the job right."

Apart from the pride that goes along with such a presumption, there is something that is overlooked. God, in fact, *did* create a world in which human beings, beginning with Adam and Eve, were not to experience any suffering. The Garden of Eden was Paradise. God created the first human beings with neither death nor disease in His plans.

But, as we know from our reading of *Genesis*, things did not work out according to God's original plan. Our primal parents could not leave well enough alone. Because they were free, they could reject the Paradise God gave them. They wanted more than was possible; they wanted to be equal to God.

Naturally, a creature cannot be both a creature and a Creator at the same time. But freedom does not necessarily choose what is realistic. The presence of pride makes it possible for freedom to lean toward the irrational and the unrealistic. Suffering, so often, is the inescapable consequence of a person refusing to be what he is. If a person overeats, smokes too much, or drinks excessively, the biological laws inherent in his body are unforgiving. He will suffer in one way or another. If a child runs away from home, he becomes homeless. If a creature severs his friendship with God, he embarks on a path of inevitable suffering, just as if he decided not to eat, breathe, or sleep. The Fall brings suffering, as does the turbulent journey back home.

Suffering is not God's idea of how man should live. We see in many instances that it is the inevitable result of man stubbornly rejecting his own nature. Of course, there are instances of suffering, like brain tumours, that defy an explanation by us. But quite often, it is the fate portrayed in Aesop's fable about the horse that, in trying to sing like a nightingale, lost its ability to whinny like a horse.

It is most interesting that when a person presumes to act as if he were God, then he would not permit suffering. But in fact when people do have an opportunity to create, they often make sure their characters suffer both continuously and immensely. For example, consider the very popular drama known as a "soap opera." It is a purely human creation written by talented writers. It characteristically and routinely depicts human life as a Hell on earth. A "soap" without a healthy sprinkling of scandalous activity simply cannot survive in the war for television ratings. Most viewers, unfortunately, prefer to diet on a menu that features vice and violence. The following is a synopsis of one week of the production known as "One Life to Live." My own survey leads me to believe that what is portrayed in these episodes is typical of such dramas.

Here is the synopsis: After bugging Peter's hospital room, Brad discovered Karen and Marco switched Mary with Jenny's deceased child. Bo questioned Asa's new security system at Olympia's crypt, where Pat and Cliff snooped. Ted tried to turn Vicky against Becky. Wanda filled Clint in on Niki Smith. Marco, who grew more restless, told Karen they would make a nifty couple. Corky, Peter's nurse, made eyes at Brad. Will advised Katrina to work on improving her self-esteem. Marcello drank away his confusion over Katrina and Dorian.

The above was created by the writers as a normal slice of life. We see immoral characters inflicting suffering on one another. Those who write such episodes have in mind an audience with an insatiable appetite for such depictions. Both the creators and the audience are living in and feeding on behaviour that is Godless. To revel in such depictions is to accept these Godless values as one's own.

We have been reflecting on perhaps the most notorious of this kind of drama — the afternoon soap opera. But evening entertainment can be equally Godless. If a person establishes his ideals on the purely secular and materialistic values that are the principal ingredients of such Media entertainment, then he should not be surprised if spiritual values become insipid or non-existent in his life. The Godless world around us is not a harmless reality. No wonder youngsters who are exposed to this kind of motivational diet lose any attraction for spiritual things, stop going to church, and do not bother to have their children baptised.

An unplugged lamp does not shine. A rebellious creature, disconnected from God, does not thrive. A chain of suffering can be inaugurated by one's own actions that are not what God intended. Addiction to violence makes goodness seem boring.

G. K. Chesterton once quipped that if there were no God, there would be no atheists. Even the existence of an atheist is an astonishing fact that the atheist himself is reluctant to acknowledge. He is too enamoured with this atheism (something that is truly his alone) to credit God for his existence. In this context, we should distinguish between professed atheists and practical atheists — those who live in a Godless way with no spiritual values guiding their daily choices.

According to the great satirist, Jonathan Swift, "That the universe was formed by a fortuitous concourse of atoms, I will no more believe than that the accidental jumbling of the alphabet would fall into a most ingenious treatise of philosophy."

Atheism is unrealistic on several counts. Many an atheist thinks he could do a better job if he were God. Yet, we have invincible difficulties in finding a person who can properly run a country, or a city, or even a small town bank properly. Let us not talk about running the cosmos. None of us could do any better that Goethe's "sorcerer's apprentice." Atheism is about pride, not logic. Theism is about love. Pride and love are mutually exclusive. But love is infinitely more realistic.

How Bad Ideas Can Be Building Blocks for the Culture of Death

—Introduction—

The strict relativist holds that no ideas are discernibly anchored in truth. A logical corollary of this tenet is that all ideas are equal. A radical egalitarianism of ideas is a direct result of epistemological relativism. One might say that all ideas are equal insofar as they are ideas. But it cannot be maintained that they are all equal insofar as they are equally commensurate with truth. Before the facts are known, all bets at the track are merely conjecture. But when the race is run and the results are in, conjecture is replaced by truth. A better would love to get a copy of tomorrow's newspaper to learn the winner in advance of the race. So too, a philosopher would love to learn how various ideas relate to truth. The winning idea is the idea that correlates with truth. In the dark, all guesses are equal. But in the light, knowledge is born, and guesses, like the darkness itself, are quickly dispelled.

A key is designed to open a lock. We know that the right key will unlock the door, while the wrong keys will not. We have no qualms about differentiating between the "right" key and the "wrong" key. And just as one key opens the lock while the others do not; some ideas reflect truth while others have no real relationship with it. Therefore, with respect to their degrees of commensurability with truth, some ideas are "right," while others are "wrong." Mortimer Adler has written two books elaborating this point: *Six Great Ideas* and *Ten Philosophical Mistakes*. There are relatively few "great ideas"; the number of not-so-great ideas is inestimable.

Philosophy, of course, is inspired by a love of wisdom. And it belongs to wisdom to distinguish between ideas that are right from those that are wrong, or, in the terminology of Kierkegaard, "reality" from "illusion." When we speak of a "bad idea," we add to a mere "wrong idea" the notion of negative practical repercussion. Thus, the notion that man is merely material is a bad idea since its implementation results in treating a being who, in truth, has spirituality and dignity, as if he were only a thing and therefore improperly, abusively, and unjustly. In order to deal with man properly, it is imperative to understand him in his truth. Relativistic humanism inevitably becomes false humanism. True humanism must be founded on the truth of man. Jacques Maritain's book, *True Humanism*, may be the definitive treatment of this issue.

The foregoing essay elaborates four bad ideas. These ideas have been selected because of the significant role they have played in the establishment of the Culture of Death that permeates the contemporary world. The reality of truth, elusive to our grasp as it sometimes may be, invalidates any basis for relativism. Ideas are not equal. Moreover, as Richard Weaver has adequately and eloquently explained in his book, *Ideas Have Consequences*, there is a price to pay or a benefit to be reaped as a direct result of whatever ideas we put into practice. Marion Montgomery's work, *The Truth of Things: Liberal Arts and The Recovery of Reality* reiterates and reinforces the same point.

In our book, *Architects of the Culture of Death*, Benjamin Wiker and I have presented a wide variety of thinkers, twenty-three in all, who have played a major role in building the present Culture of Death. In this essay, I will be concentrating more on the bricks than the builders, the ideas more than the ideologues. The four bad ideas that provide the underlying structure for the foregoing essay are the following:

1. Will as Absolute
2. Society as Perfectible
3. Pleasure as Paramount
4. Adversity as Unbearable

—Will as Absolute—

When will is made absolute, reason is extinguished. The world in which will reigns in the absence of reason is utterly terrifying. There is no rational defense against will unleashed.

The first philosopher to depict will in this terrifying manner was Arthur Schopenhauer (1788-1860). Throughout the history of philosophy, dating back to Plato and reinforced by the Judeo-Christian tradition, philosophers viewed reality as intelligible to human reason. In contrast, Schopenhauer believed that the core of reality is will, "a blind incessant impulse."[17] "Will is the thing-in-itself, the inner content, the essence of the world."[18] It is the "primordial being" (*Urwesen*), the "primordial source" of that which is (*Urquelle des Seinden*), the prime mover of all activity. It has no goal outside of itself and its gratuitous action. It is found everywhere, in the pull of gravitation, the crystallization of rocks, the movements of the stars and planets, the appetites of brute animals, and the volitions of man. This unwieldy and pervasive force, for Schopenhauer, manifests itself as Nature. It is futile for an individual to fight against this force, since it has no regard for him and is bent on his ultimate destruction. Nature, the very embodiment of will, is destined to destroy the very individuals it wills into existence.[19]

Schopenhauer's impact on modernity, especially in regard to dissociating reason from will, is inestimable. According to Thomas Mann, "Schopenhauer, as psychologist of the will, is the father of all modern psychology. From him the line runs, by way of the psychological radicalism of Nietzsche, straight to Freud and the men who built up the psychology of the unconscious and applied it to mental science."[20] And Karl Stern contends that, "one can trace a direct descent from the irredeemable non-reason of Schopenhauer's 'will' to that incomprehensible phase of madness in this century that nearly succeeded in destroying the world."[21] Yet, the "madness" seems to continue unabated.

For Friedrich Nietzsche, who read Schopenhauer avidly, it becomes "the will to power." For Sigmund Freud, it lodges in the instinctive power of the "libido." Wilhelm Reich locates it at the "irrational core of sexual desire." Jean-Paul Sartre finds it everywhere in nature and experiences it in the form of "nausea." Madame de Beauvoir is sickened by the way it "suffocated women biologically" and makes them its easy prey. Elisabeth Badinter seeks to escape from its "oppressiveness" by escaping into an "absolutized Ego." Schopenhauer is the Father of a legacy in modern philosophy known as "Vitalistic Irrationality."[22] It is a legacy, Manichaean in essence, that reacts with horror at the presence of Nature, the irrational tool of a merciless will.

There is a direct line from Schopenhauer to the attitude of will without reason that lies at the heart of the pro-choice movement. Judith Jarvis Thomson, whose "A Defense of Abortion"[23] is the most widely reprinted essay not only on the subject of abortion, but in all of contemporary philosophy, is a direct descendent of Arthur Schopenhauer. She likens pregnancy to an invasion of "people seeds," a child growing to gigantic proportions at an extraordinary rate, or being hooked up against one's will to the kidney's of a violinist. Philosopher John T. Wilcox sees Thomson's terrifying notions of pregnancy as comparable with a concept of Nature that is "demonic" and "malevolent."[24] For Wilcox, Thomson regards "nature as demonic, out to get you, violating your rights as you innocently go about your business."[25]

The notion of will as absolute has an equally disturbing corollary in the form of "freedom as absolute." This latter notion characterizes the heart of Jean-Paul Sartre's philosophy and has had a decisive influence on many writers, including Simone de Beauvoir and Ayn Rand.

For Sartre, man is so free that he is not even a man. Therefore, "existence precedes essence," since any essence would constitute a limitation of his freedom. Freedom without limitation is unrealistic. But when it is exercised as much as it can be, it proves destructive.

—Society as Perfectible—

From time to time the belief spreads that a perfect society can be constructed, that imperfect man can be made perfect through imperfect means. The Spanish existentialist, José Ortega y Gasset has stated that "an idea framed without any other object than that of perfecting it as an idea, however it may conflict with reality, is precisely what is called utopia."

There are two immensely influential utopianist thinkers in the modern world who believed passionately that the state did not exist for man, but man existed for the state. These utopianists, Karl Marx (1818-1883) and Auguste Comte (1798-1857) were radically different in how they viewed the means that must be employed in order to realize their utopian dreams.

For Marx, violence is inevitable. "When our turn comes," he wrote, "we shall not disguise our terrorism."[26] Comte, a naïve sentimentalist, believed that he could exploit people's feelings about love. "Love is my principle, Order is my basis, Progress is my aim," he wrote. [27]

Neither Marx nor Comte believed either in God or in the dignity of the individual person. For Marx, individuals are absorbed into a class. In *Das Kapital* he writes, "I speak of individuals insofar as they are personifications of special classes of relations and interests." One special class, the "ruling class" was at war with another special class, the "working class." Classes were homogeneous and engaged in a necessary dialectical struggle with adversarial classes. Class struggle, violence, and revolution were all necessary.

Comte, who detested traditional religions, sought a new religion of Positivism in which the "slaves of God" would be transformed into the "servants of humanity." "Let there be no dissembling the fact," Comte writes, "that today the servants of Humanity are ousting the servants of God."[28] Comte worked indefatigably and at long length in designing his "social physics" according to which his followers would submit blindly to him as their supreme dictator. He envisioned selfless souls who have no personal rights worshipping Humanity itself.

Neither Marx nor Comte grasped the unity of the human person. They saw him as merely fodder for the collective, bereft of soul, devoid of any individual significance. Since they believed the state was more important than the individual soul, they both employed, though through radically different techniques, a Procrustean methodology in the vain attempt to make imperfect man fit the mold of what they believed to be a perfect idea.

The results, as history has shown, have been disastrous. Man cannot find happiness and fulfillment while he denies the unique character of his personality.

—Pleasure as Paramount—

Wilhelm Reich (1897-1957) studied medicine at Vienna University. In 1922, Sigmund Freud selected him to be a first assistant physician for his newly formed Psychoanalytic-Polyclinic. He was also an avid student of Marxism. In 1930, he left his Vienna and went to Berlin where he became an active member of the German Communist Party.

His affections for Freud and Marx were not without critical reflection. He knew that Freud had no politics and that Marx had no psychology. He was also convinced that society was both sick and unjust. He wanted to provide a grand therapy that would not only cure individuals from their private afflictions, but also heal society from its own social pathologies. In order to do this, he felt it was necessary to combine Freudianism and Marxism into a single therapeutic so that he could free the individual from his repressions as well as society from its cultural inhibitions.

So it was, that Reich became the world's first Freudo-Marxist. Since he felt that by themselves, neither Freud nor Marx could provide the comprehensive therapy that the world needed, he was ultimately ejected from both Freudian and Marxist circles. Yet Reich was enthralled by the grandeur and scope of his own revolution, one he accused the Freudians and Marxists as being too timid to launch. "There can be no doubt," he exclaimed, "the sexual revolution is underway, and no power in the world will stop it." The *revolution* that Reich envisioned was far more sweeping than that of any Marxist. His war against *repression* went further than that of any Freudian. His aim was to strip away all repression, all cultural and social masks, all forms of authority, so that a total revolution would be achieved in which the real human being would emerge, whole and clean.

To achieve this, all traces of what Freud called, the "super-ego," had to be dissolved. In this regard, Reich saw "conscience" as the first "tyranny." With the dissolution of conscience, morality would also disappear, as well as any lingering voice of authority. With all this stripping away, what could possibly remain? For Reich, it was man's "primary biological impulses," the bedrock that lay at his "deep, natural core."

Jean-Jacques Rousseau had maintained that the source of all evil is civilization. He rejected the Christian notion of original sin as "blasphemy." For Rousseau, man would find his beatitude in a primitive state of innocence. Rousseau had a deep influence, not only on the "flower-children" of the sixties, but also on Reich. But Reich went further. For him, original sin is fear of self. Yet the self, for Reich, is essentially the erotic impulse, an instinct that is far below the level of either personality or community. Man begins to "armor" himself against himself at the moment he begins to think. "I think, therefore, I am neurotic" became Reich's anti-intellectual, yet self-identifying logo. He feared that the act of thinking would divide the individual, separating thought from body at the expense of his primal urges. Thinking, therefore, was a disease. The ideal character for Reich is the unafraid, unthinking individual who has "satisfied his strong libidinal needs at the risk of social ostracism."

But Reich, who, in the attempt to make pleasure paramount had to exorcise thinking, ended up a caricature of a free man. He died in a federal penitentiary while serving a two-year sentence for defrauding the American public, and having been diagnosed by a prison psychiatrist as paranoid. The man who tried to liberate people through an exclusive preoccupation with pleasure, closed out his life incarcerated and suffering from delusions of persecution.

—Adversity as Unbearable—

Three contemporary figures have been in the forefront of promoting euthanasia. They are Peter Singer (1946 -), Derek Humphry (1930 -), and Jack Kevorkian (1928 - 2011). Singer is the thinker, Humphry the publicist, and Kevorkian was the executioner. Together, this triumvirate represents the three prongs of a movement that is dedicated to the notion that death is a rational choice when life gets to be troublesome.

In his book, *Rethinking Life and Death: The Collapse of Our Traditional Ethics*, Peter Singer remarks that, "After ruling our thoughts and our decisions about life and death for nearly two thousand years, the traditional Western ethics has collapsed." [29] The old and now defunct ethics is based on the "sanctity of life." The new ethics that Singer proposes is based on "quality of life." Whereas the "sanctity of life" is carried with it the prohibition, "Thou Shall Not Kill," the new, more flexible ethic states, "Thou Mayest Kill If You Think Your Life Has Become Too Bothersome."

Championing this notion, journalist and publicist Derek Humphry claims, "We are trying to overturn 2,000 years of Christian tradition." [30] Putting these ideas into practice, Jack Kevorkian, aka "Dr. Death," by his own admission, has assisted in the deaths of 130 human beings. The majority of his victims were not terminally ill. Some, in fact, were suffering from conditions no more life threatening than loneliness, and low self-esteem. On November 27, 1998, before tens of millions of televiewers who had tuned into CBS's *60 Minutes,* Kevorkian injected fifty-two-year-old Thomas Youk with potassium chloride, thereby ending his life. Kevorkian was subsequently charged and convicted of second-degree homicide. He served eight years in prison and died in 2011, eight days after his 83rd birthday. For assisting in these "mercy killings," Humphry praised Kevorkian as a "brave and lonely pioneer."[31]

Singer, Humphry, and Kevorkian have little to say about how people can face adversity without falling into despair. The dignity of the person means nothing. It is the "preferred state" of life that counts for everything. Thus, Singer can declare, matter-of-factly, "When the death of the disabled infant will lead to the birth of another infant with better prospects of a happy life, the total amount of happiness will be greater if the disabled infant is killed."[32] Granted, it is better to be more happy than to be less happy. Yet this point hardly forms a basis for ending the life of a person who has less happiness than the hypothetically conceived greater happiness of his possible replacement. Ethics should center on the person, not the quantum of happiness a person may or may not enjoy. It is the subject who exists that has the right to life, and neither Peter Singer nor anyone else who employs a "relative happiness calculator" should expropriate that right.

Just as the utopianists subordinate the individual to the state, the euthanasiasts subordinate the individual to a state of wellbeing. In both cases, it is the abstraction that rules.

—Conclusion—

Man is one being. He is a unification of body and soul, materiality and corporeality, reason and will. His life is a composite of individuality and communality, freedom and responsibility, pleasure and adversity.

When man is fractured and asked to function without the use of all his organic powers, he becomes deprived, wounded, and ultimately incapacitated. The building bricks for the Culture of Death are merely the shards of his personality.

George Weigel, in his definitive biography of John Paul II, *Witness to Hope*, appraises the Holy Father's papacy as "a one-act drama" involving "the tension between various false humanisms that degrade the humanity they claim to defend and exalt, and the true humanism to which the biblical vision of the human person is a powerful witness."[33]

False humanisms are based on bad ideas, that is, ideas that truncate man, fractionalize him into less than he is. Man is more than the splinters of his existence each taken in isolation. *Will* must not be divorced from *reason, freedom* must not be uprooted from *responsibility, society* must not ignore the *individual person, pleasure* must not be dissociated from *conscience,* and *adversity* must be faced with *virtue.*

TRUTH AND RELATIVISM

—Relativism and Truth—

Joseph Cardinal Ratzinger's book, *Truth and Tolerance*, focuses on a widespread conflict that exists in today's world between two values that are, in the popular mind, no longer seen as complementary. This conflict is symptomatic of a deeper conflict between philosophy and politics. *Truth* belongs to the sphere of philosophy, while *tolerance* belongs to the sphere of politics. The former reveals what something is; the latter describes how people should behave toward each other in a civil society. However, so much importance is now attached to tolerance, that it has been separated from truth, which, in turn, has been relegated to the sphere of mere opinion. To state the matter quite simply: tolerance has been absolutized, while truth has been relativized.

Nonetheless, such a separation of tolerance from truth (or politics from philosophy) is *preposterous*, in the original meaning of the term. The Latin words *prae* (before) and *posterius* (after) relate to the absurd or "preposterous" practice of placing "before" that which should come "after," like putting the cart before the horse. Placing man first and God second is preposterous in the same way. But the preposterous maneuver, however, has a more sinister implication – it first eclipses what should be primary and then banishes it in the direction of oblivion. Thus, placing man first and God second soon leads to atheism; placing politics first and philosophy second leads to agnosticism, or the elimination of philosophy. [34]

The distinguished Thomistic philosopher, Etienne Gilson, has made the comment that one of the essential features of Aquinas' thinking was his ability to put things in their proper order. In philosophy this is critical, for, as Gilson explains, if an idea is out of order it is "lost, not in the usual sense that it is not to be found where you expected it to be, but in the much more radical sense that it is no longer to be found anywhere."[35] One of the more urgent problems in the modern world is the recovery of philosophy (and truth along with it) so that we understand how various realities relate to each other, whether they be God and man, philosophy and politics, the state and its citizens.

The reason, according to Ratzinger, for the exaggerated importance given to tolerance and its promotion over truth, rests on the fact that we now live in a pluralistic world consisting of a wide diversity of values, customs, and religious beliefs. How, then, is it possible for people to live in harmony with each other and be tolerant toward each other's differences? If truth is invoked, it would presumably have the insidious effect of making one group appear superior to another and consequently intolerant. The answer to this problem has been the adoption of *relativism* and its concomitant removal of a philosophy that is anchored in truth.

Ratzinger fully understands the dire consequences resulting from excising truth from politics and making relativism sovereign. "Relativism," he writes, "in certain aspects has become the real religion of modern man."[36] It represents, he goes on to say, "the most profound difficulty of our day."[37] These austere words cannot be taken lightly, for the Cardinal is a careful thinker and not given to hyperbole.

The experiment in trying to be tolerant in the absence of any regulatory truth has proven to be a failure. It has inevitably led to a decisive intolerance of the Catholic Church, for example, and not because She opposes tolerance, but because She refuses to accord it a higher status than truth. In other words, the Church insists that all things be placed in their proper order. This is enough for the world to indict Her for being "intolerant." Ratzinger asks the pertinent question, "what meaning does belief then have, what positive meaning does religion have, if it cannot be connected with truth?"[38]

A pagan philosopher answered this very question better than two millennia ago. Marcus Tullius Cicero, in the year 44 B.C., reasoned that religion without truth is merely superstition. "We should do ourselves and our countrymen a great deal of good," he wrote in his treatise, *On Divination*, "if we were to root superstition out entirely." But the great statesman and philosopher, mindful of the human proclivity to throw the baby out with the bathwater, was quick to assert that he did "not want religion destroyed along with superstition." He urged the abolition of superstition, but the retention of religion. We do not need superstition, he proposed, but we do need religion. The distinguishing factor, for Cicero, was natural science that revealed the truth of things. "That there is some eternal Being," he wrote, "who stands out above the rest, and that the human race ought to serve and admire Him, is an admission that the beauty of the universe and the orderliness of the celestial bodies compels us to make. Therefore, just as religion, being associated with natural science, ought actually to be propagated, so every root of superstition ought to be weeded out."[39] Simply stated, Cicero enjoined his fellow countrymen to use truth as a way of distinguishing religion from what he deemed not worth tolerating, namely superstition.

The 20th Century American philosopher Mortimer Adler, reiterates Cicero's position in his book, *Truth in Religion: The*

Plurality of Religions and the Unity of Truth. He acknowledges that truth is needed to support religion as its preamble, but also points out that without truth there can be neither unity nor peace: "A great epoch in the history of mankind lies ahead of us in the millennium. It will not begin until there is a universal acknowledgement of the unity of truth in all areas of culture to which the standard of truth is applicable; for only then will all men be able to live together peacefully in a world of cultural community under one government. Only then will world civilization and world history begin."[40]

In an earlier work, *Six Great Ideas*, Dr. Adler distinguishes between the ideas we judge by (Truth, Goodness, and Beauty) and the ideas we live by (Liberty, Equality, and Justice). His basic point is that we cannot enjoy Liberty, Equality, and Justice (ideas that virtually everyone endorses enthusiastically) unless we know something about Truth, Goodness, and Beauty. For example, there can be no justice without truth. In the absence of truth, no verdict (*verum* + *dicere* – to tell the truth) can be delivered that separates the guilty from the innocent or justice from injustice. It is a profoundly sad irony in the modern world that people are willing to ignore the very means that is indispensable for producing what they most ardently desire. They shun truth and expect justice to flower in a barren desert.

Marcello Pera, a non-believer, describes the present situation in the West as anything but the tranquility that arises from mutual tolerance, but as a "prison-house of insincerity and hypocrisy known as political correctness."[41] People live in constant fear that any gesture or statement suggesting that one thing might be better than another is not only *not* tolerated, but met with scorn, derision, and often severe reprisals. As Pera avers, "The adjective 'better' is forbidden."[42]

Philosophy, it should be emphasized, is not a luxury for the elite or an idol game indulged in at universities. Philosophy, because it is properly concerned with truth, goodness, beauty, and other fundamental verities, is indispensable in providing the basis for civilization and all the benefits that flow from it, including unity, civility, justice, peace, art, and science. By setting tolerance above truth, tolerance degenerates into intolerance, while truth is abandoned altogether. The result is akin to what Plato describes in the opening of the seventh chapter of his *Republic*: cave dwellers who are intolerant of education, mesmerized by shadows, and closed to the light of truth that could improve their lives. The rejection of truth does not make people tolerant. As the great Catholic philosopher, Jacques Maritain has stated, "the man who says 'What is truth?' as Pilate did, is not a tolerant man, but a betrayer of the human race."[43]

Tolerance can hardly be the first principle of human conduct. And it has never been the founding principle of any civilization. The Judeo-Christian God commands us to love, not to be tolerant. Tolerance is not a first step or pro-active; it is acquiescence, capitulation to something to which one neither approves nor disapproves. It presupposes moral neutrality. It is a response, not an initiative, leaving the question, "response to *what*?" unanswered. When it is used as a first principle, it soon contradicts itself. The Spanish government, in the interest of expressing tolerance to married couples of the same sex who have adopted children, has replaced the "offensive" terms "father" and "mother" on birth certificates with "Progenitor A" and "Progenitor B." What is initially tolerance toward same-sex couples soon becomes intolerance toward the very words "father" and "mother." Similarly the BBC ordered its writers to avoid the contentious terms, "husband" and "wife." Many North American universities have outlawed student pro-life groups in the interest of demonstrating their tolerance toward those who are "pro-choice."

One cannot simultaneously tolerate contraries and contradictories. Opposition to same-sex marriage is not tolerated and routinely denounced as "homophobic." To cite but one salient example, in January 2006, the European Parliament passed a resolution condemning states that do not recognize same-sex marriages as "homophobic." The implication here is that expressing a philosophical opinion on this matter is not only discriminatory, but also indicative of a psychological disorder. Relativism that is the underpinning of an out-of-control political correctness conveys the message that human beings are fundamentally incapable of grasping the truth of things, that they would rather fight than think.

It is more than a bit ridiculous to ask a man who is about to be boiled in a pot and eaten, at a purely religious feast, why he does not maintain a relativistic view toward all religions. The mind, and even the heart, may entertain absurdities, but it is most unlikely that one would continue denying reality when his nervous system calls his instinct for self-preservation to attention.[44] A relativist cannot afford to get too close to reality.

Relativism is a default philosophy that emerges as a result of an unwillingness to put truth and tolerance in their proper order. But it is unworkable on a practical level and creates immense, though unnecessary stumbling blocks in the path of *education, democracy*, and the implementation of the *natural law*. In fact, it contributes, significantly, to the *Culture of Death*.

—Relativism and Education—

Allan Bloom's *The Closing of the American Mind* is a sustained critique of higher education in the United States, specifically, the widespread relativism that effectively suppresses the proper openness needed to distinguish between right and wrong, true and false, good and evil. The author begins the Introduction of his tome, one that remained on the *New York Times* best-seller list for more than 30 weeks, by declaring that, "There is one thing a professor can be absolutely certain of: almost every student entering the university believes, or says he believes, that truth is relative."[45] Such students, according to Professor Bloom, assume that their belief in relativism is axiomatic and beyond questioning. They are, so to speak, not open to their own closedness. As a consequence, there is little if any thinking going on about their first principles. "These are things you don't think about,"[46] laments the University of Chicago philosophy professor.

Relativism does away with the need to think. After all, if the mind cannot know truth, and all opinions warrant equal respect, why struggle to comprehend the incomprehensible? No rational justification is needed to defend any relativistic position. Like Ray Bradbury's 1953 novella, *Fahrenheit 451*, where firemen start fires instead of putting them out, universities now use relativism to prevent thinking rather than to encourage it.

The Pontifical Council for Culture has addressed this peculiar phenomenon of schools not teaching students how to think in a 2006 study that flies under the sesquipedalian title of "The Christian Faith at the Dawn of the New Millennium and the Challenge of Unbelief and Religious Indifference." One of its main conclusions is "the urgency of learning to think, from school to university."

It may appear surprising to some that the Catholic Church, known primarily for her foundation in faith, is taking up the role of teaching people how to think. Yet the phenomenon of not thinking, especially about crucial matters, is pandemic — both within and outside of the Church — and often goes unchallenged.

What, we might well ask, are those people who have not yet learned to think using as a substitute for thinking? In a word, they are *reacting*. They react affirmatively to the settled opinions of the day that they themselves have not settled in their own minds. They parrot ideas that are trendy, media-approved, and politically correct. Not only that, but they bundle their collection of unexamined ideas and wrap them up in a package they claim to be a "philosophy."

And this "philosophy," as we have noted, is Relativism, one that cries out for an urgent reexamination. According to the tenets of this "philosophy," truth either does not exist or is unattainable. As a result, since there is no reliable anchor that can ground opinions in reality, all opinions have equal merit. What is assumed to be the democratization of philosophy is really its destruction.

Relativists, despite their rejection of any sure connection with reality, are not averse to referring to what they believe to be reality in order to buttress their position. Einstein's "Theory of Relativity" is often called upon to substantiate the notion that "everything is relative." The Media has been more than eager in promoting the contradictory notion that there is an objective basis for asserting that nothing is objective. For example, the September 24, 1979 issue of *Time* carried a full-page advertisement that stated, in bold-faced letters and under a picture of Einstein: EVERYTHING IS RELATIVE.[47]

While we cannot expect people in general to understand the intricacies and complexities of Einstein's theory, we can know enough about it to be confident that neither Einstein nor his celebrated theory are the least bit relativistic. As the great physicist himself avers, in language that calls to mind Aristotle and Aquinas, "Belief in an external world independent of the perceiving subject is the basis of all natural science."[48] As far as his theory is concerned, let us consider the words of Fr. Stanley Jaki: "Einstein's Theory of Relativity is the most absolutist theory ever proposed in the history of science. In fact, the entire success of Einstein's theory is that it is absolutist. According to it, the value of the speed of light is independent of any reference systems and therefore has a value which is absolutely valid."[49]

Initially, Einstein thought of calling his theory "The Theory of Invariance," because the speed of light, the "hitching-post" of the universe, is constant (or invariant). Time and motion are relative, but all that means for Einstein is that they are related to something that is not relative.

When philosophy was in its infancy, an imaginative thinker explained how the earth was sustained in space by postulating that it rested on the back of a tortoise. The question inevitably shifted to "what holds up the tortoise"? "Why, another tortoise," someone answered. "And what holds up the second tortoise," someone else queried? "Well," said a pundit, "it's tortoises all the way down!" Such a response is not philosophical but facetious. Philosophy is supposed to culminate in wisdom, not foolishness.

Relativists are fond of alluding to the timeless aphorism, *De gustibus non disputandum est* (concerning taste, there must be no dispute). But they ignore the more important aphorism, *De veritate disputandum est* (concerning truth, we must engage in dispute). Engaging in dispute is evidence of thinking. And we must engage in dispute, that is, involving ourselves in trying to figure out what is true and what is not true, because of the simple fact that *the truth matters*. To avoid thinking, no matter how convenient and time saving that may be, is intellectually derelict and morally irresponsible.

Pope Benedict XVI has given some popular currency to the phrase, "The Dictatorship of Relativism." The true relativist (if there could be one) would have nothing to dictate to anyone. He would be utterly deferential and completely respectful even of opinions that contradicted his own. The fact that relativists can aspire to the role of dictator is a good indication that it is impossible for anyone to purge himself entirely of his connections with reality.

The ancient sophist Pyrrho of Ellis, who had the reputation of not being sure of anything, was once observed fleeing from a rabid dog. Bystanders ridiculed his behavior that obviously repudiated his philosophy. Pyrrho's meek response conveyed an inescapable truth: "It is difficult to get away entirely from nature."

Something is relative when it corresponds to two fixed points. Between the reality of a woman and her son are the relationships of mother and child. The woman is the child's mother, and he is her son. They are related to each other. Mortimer Adler, a Thomistic philosopher who entered the Church in his nineties, would have heartily endorsed the Pontifical Council for Culture's commitment to helping people to learn how to think. For thinking rightly leads to truth, and truth is the only avenue to peace. In what is perhaps his best known work, *How to Read a Book*, Adler reiterates the time-honored point that the Liberal Arts are truly liberating because they liberate the student *through* reason not *from* it. "The liberal who frees himself *from* reason," he writes, "rather than *through* it, surrenders to the only other arbiter in human affairs – force, or what Mr. Chamberlain has called 'the awful arbitrament of war'."[50] Adler's recognition that relativism leads to the imposition of force is perfectly consistent with Pope Benedict's oft-repeated reference to the "Dictatorship of Relativism." If people are not moved voluntarily by reason and truth, they will be moved involuntarily by power and force.

—Relativism and Democracy—

The original title of Allan Bloom's best-seller was not as catchy as "The Closing of the American Mind," but it was no less accurate in capturing the book's central thesis – "How Higher Education Has Failed Democracy and Impoverished the Souls of Today's Students." The good professor understood that it is set in the eternal order of things for a good education to be both a foundation and a safeguard for good democracy. Moreover, a good education does not neglect the indispensable importance of truth and virtue. To the extent that we abolish the role of truth and virtue in education, we will suffer as a political entity.

Pope Benedict XVI has reiterated the point that ethical relativism cannot be the basis for democracy, nor can it bring about tolerance and mutual respect.[51] In the absence of virtuous people, he states, democracy yields to totalitarian interests. He views with no small amount of apprehension that "Relativism thus also appears as being the philosophical basis of democracy."[52]

Ethical relativism cannot possibly be the basis for a good democracy because it is inherently incapable of providing a blueprint for unity or an inspiration for decency. Nor can it provide a basis for either tolerance or mutual respect.

The noted Harvard sociologist, Gordon Allport, worked on his classic study, *The Nature of Prejudice*, during the aftermath of World War II. This was a period of high unemployment and widespread hunger throughout the civilized world that was further burdened by pervasive cynicism and nervous insecurity. It was not a climate in which people were eager to embrace the democratic ideal. Rather, it was a time when people fell prey to demagogues who were only too eager to wrap them in a pseudo-protective blanket of totalitarianism.

In times of uncertainty, people often chose not the moral ideal, but the quick solution to their immediate needs. "It was a stuporous error," wrote Allport, a man not given to using words recklessly, "for the western world to believe that democratic ideology, stemming from Judeo-Christian ethics and reinforced by political creeds of many nations, would itself gradually overspread the world."[53]

"Democracy, we now realize," Allport went on to say, somewhat mournfully, "places burdens upon the personality sometimes too great to bear." Do we continue to realize what Allport thought people realized better than a half-century ago? And what does a person need in order to bear such heavy burdens? It is apparently something we have forgotten. In a word, for the Harvard sociologist, it is "virtue." "The maturely democratic person," he wrote, "must possess subtle virtues."[54]

Thomas Paine knew about this around the time of the American Revolution. The author of *Common Sense* advised his countrymen that, "When we are planning for posterity, we ought to remember that virtue is not hereditary."

The democratic ideal has proven to be less exportable to countries such as Iraq, Afghanistan, and Iran, than arms, coffee, and computers because it presupposes the cultivation of the many virtues that are needed to make democracy a practical reality. There is no point in exporting lamps to a nation that has no electricity.

A few years ago, in an address to the United Nations, John Paul II reiterated that "democracy requires wisdom and virtue: it stands or falls with the truths it embodies and promotes." On this occasion, however (October 8, 2002), the country that was forefront in the Holy Father's mind was not a nation of the Middle East, but America herself.

In this light, the problem of exporting democracy becomes even more difficult. The initial problem lies in a nation's lack of preparedness in receiving it; the second problem involves first advertising and then trying to export a tainted product. If America is losing her affection for virtue, particularly the subtle virtues needed for democracy, such as selflessness, a desire for truth, a willingness to work, a keen sense of justice and fair play, respect for marriage and the family, and reverence for God, it is losing hold of her own democratic ideal. And one cannot give what one does not have.

True democracy is surely a worthy attainment. And we should never forget that countless souls have fought and died to keep it from perishing. But at the moment, we sorely underestimate how much it demands in the currency of moral virtue, and how easy it can dissipate when it is taken for granted. John Court-

ney Murray has remarked that "men [once] thought that democracy was inevitable; now they know that it is an achievement,
always precarious."

Exporting democracy can succeed only to the degree that
its recipients have cultivated enough virtue (and to a sufficient-
ly high degree) so that they can take on its burdens and work to
see it prosper. America may have forgotten something of her own
history. As her fourth president, James Madison, once declared,
"To suppose that any form of government will secure liberty or
happiness without any virtue in the people is a chimerical idea."
Democracy is a living thing, and as such, must be continuously
nourished and vigorously exercised. America's first concern, in
the realm of politics, then, is the health of its own democracy. And
moral virtue is the lifeblood of that health.

—Relativism and the Natural Law—

Pope Benedict XVI told members of the International Theological Commission, in an early October 2007 address, that the
natural law must be the foundation of democracy, so that those in
power are not given the chance to determine what is good or evil.

We human beings, of course, cannot "determine" what is
good or evil in the strict sense of the term. Our lot is one of "discovery" rather than determination. There is an old Walt Disney
song from the movie, *Lady and the Tramp*, in which two animated
cats pay respect to the rigorous continuity of the natural order of
things: "We are Siamese if you please. We are Siamese if you
don't please." Being a Siamese cat is a reality that is established
independently of external opinion. Disney's oriental felines are
not relativists in any sense. They know who they are and really
do not care what other people might think or say. They stubbornly
"purr-sist," if the reader will pardon the pun, in being who they

are. They illustrate the maxim that the order of naming should always conform to the order of being.

There are certain goods that are as essential to democracy as being Siamese is to a Siamese cat. They include, as Pope Benedict enumerates, "human dignity, human life, the institution of the family and the equity of the social order." These essentials, he avers, have been clouded over so that "skepticism and ethical relativism" threaten to undermine the foundations of democracy and a just social order. The mistaken belief prevails that relativism offers "tolerance."[55] The truth of the matter, however, is that relativism leaves people vulnerable to those in power who determine that something is whatever they want it to be. Thus, the human unborn are referred to as merely "tissue," while elderly people who are incapacitated are said to be in a "vegetative state."

In appealing to the natural law, the Holy Father is affirming a rich philosophical tradition. In stating that the natural law is "the norm written by the Creator in man's heart," he is not being theologically narrow, but philosophically broad. It is a tradition that embraces the thought of Cicero, the Stoics, the great moralists of antiquity, as well as the great dramatists. Antigone, the eponymous heroine of Sophocles' play appeals to her king to honor "The unchangeable unwritten code of Heaven." Antigone remains, according to Jacques Maritain, "the eternal heroine of the natural law."[56]

The natural law can be ignored, disregarded, contradicted, or misunderstood; but it cannot be either changed or broken. It is rooted in who we are as human beings, taking into consideration our natural inclinations to act in accordance with what contributes to our fulfillment and happiness. Perhaps Jacques Maritain has expressed it most accurately and concisely when he speaks of "an order or a disposition which human reason can discern and according to which the human will must act in order to attune itself to the necessary ends of the human being. The unwritten law, or natural law, is nothing more than that."[57]

Aquinas pointed out in the First Book of his *Summa Theologica* that there are two senses in which a thing is said to be natural. The first is a matter of necessity, such as the upward movement of fire. [58] The second is an inclination that, in order to fulfill its end, requires reason's discovery and the will's affirmation. The Angelic Doctor then states that matrimony and political life exemplify the natural law in this sense. Consequently, there is an important difference between the "laws of nature" that operate out of necessity, and the "natural law" that requires the use of reason and the assent of the will.

One might say that the entire historic drama of man lies in whether or not he will heed the natural law or vainly attempt to live by his own prerogatives. Benedict, therefore, is not overstating his point when he proclaims, "The advance of individuals and of society along the path of true progress depends upon respect for natural moral law, in conformity with right reason, which is participation in the eternal reason of God."[59]

Benedict, pope and theologian, is, ironically, making an appeal that is more politically democratic than what passes for democracy in most of today's polities. He is advising everyone that it is far better to live in accordance with our natural inclinations than to relativize real, natural values, and delegate to some the power to rule, not wisely, but as they wish. In so stating this point, he is in full accord with Vatican II: "The Catholic Church is by the will of Christ the teacher of truth. It is her duty to proclaim and teach with authority the truth which is Jesus Christ and, at the same time, to declare and confirm by her authority the principles of the good moral order which spring from nature itself."[60]

—Relativism and the Culture of Death—

In his encyclical letter, *Evangelium Vitae* (The Culture of Life), John Paul II asks how, what he terms a "Culture of Death," came about. One contributing factor he mentions is "the profound crisis of culture, which generates skepticism in relation to the very foundations of knowledge and ethics."[61] Skepticism is the attitude of uncertainty that breeds relativism as its logical philosophical expression. Skepticism is the parent of relativism, the "bad seed," one might say.

Cardinal Ratzinger, in his book, *On the Way to Jesus Christ,* once again bemoans "the relativizing of ethical values,"[62] but also points out how "taking unrestricted pleasure in life . . . leads straight to the culture of death."[63] Skepticism and relativism are not friends of truth. And when truth is removed from the equation, they welcome and give an established place to harmful ideas that contribute directly to the Culture of Death.

The strict relativist, as we have been pointing out, holds that no ideas are discernibly anchored in truth. A logical corollary of this tenet is that all ideas are equal. A radical egalitarianism of ideas, therefore, is a direct result of such epistemological relativism. One might say that all ideas are equal insofar as they are ideas. But it cannot be maintained that they are all equal insofar as they are equally commensurate with truth. Before the facts are known, all bets at the track are merely conjecture. But when the race is run and the results are in, conjecture is replaced by truth. A bettor would love nothing more than to get a copy of tomorrow's newspaper to learn the winner in advance of the race. So too, a philosopher would love to learn how various ideas relate to truth. The winning idea is the idea that correlates with truth. In the dark, all guesses are equal. But in the light, knowledge is born, and guesses, like the darkness itself, are quickly dispelled.

A key is designed to open a lock. We know that the right

key will unlock the door, while the wrong keys will not. We have no qualms about differentiating between the "right" key and the "wrong" key. And just as one key opens the lock while the others do not, some ideas reflect truth while others have no real relationship with it. Therefore, with respect to their degrees of commensurability with truth, some ideas are "right," while others are "wrong." Mortimer Adler's books *Six Great Ideas* and *Ten Philosophical Mistakes* well illustrate this point. There are relatively few "great ideas"; the number of not-so-great ideas is inestimable.

Philosophy, of course, is inspired by a love of wisdom. And it belongs to wisdom to distinguish between ideas that are right from those that are wrong, or, in the terminology of Kierkegaard, "reality" from "illusion." When we speak of a "bad idea," we add to a mere "wrong idea" the notion of negative practical repercussion. Thus, the notion that man is merely material is a bad idea since its implementation results in treating a being who, in truth, has spirituality and dignity, as if he were only a thing and therefore improperly, abusively, and unjustly. In order to deal with man properly, it is imperative to understand him in his truth. Relativistic humanism inevitably becomes false humanism. True humanism must be founded on the truth of man. Jacques Maritain's book, *True Humanism*, may be the definitive treatment on this issue.

—Conclusion—

Man is one being. He is a unification of body and soul, materiality and corporeality, reason and will. His life is a composite of individuality and communality, freedom and responsibility, pleasure and adversity.

When man is fractured and asked to function without the use of all his organic powers, he becomes deprived, wounded, and ultimately incapacitated. The building blocks for the Culture of

Death are merely the shards of his personality. The house of cards they construct soon falls, as it inevitably must.

George Weigel, in his definitive biography of John Paul II, *Witness to Hope*, appraises the Holy Father's papacy as "a one-act drama" involving "the tension between various false humanisms that degrade the humanity they claim to defend and exalt, and the true humanism to which the biblical vision of the human person is a powerful witness."[64]

False humanisms are based on bad ideas, that is, ideas that truncate man, fractionalize him into less than he is. Man is more than the splinters of his existence where each splinter is taken in isolation. *Will* must not be divorced from *reason, freedom* must not be uprooted from *responsibility, society* must not ignore the individual person, *pleasure* must not be dissociated from *conscience,* and *adversity* must be faced with virtue. Briefly, no reality can be separated from its concomitant truth.

Relativism, as we have tried to elucidate, represents the failure to come to terms with truth, particularly the truth of the human being as a person. It puts aside that which, by nature, is primary, namely, man as a seeker of truth and a builder of civilization. It omits the blueprint and attempts to construct a house that cannot stand. The collapsing of this house leaves us with a Culture of Death.

The enveloping Culture of Death poses a daunting challenge for Christians. And yet, it is Christianity itself that holds the only solution to the current problem. Christopher Dawson offers us a needed ray of hope as he reminds us of our rich and redeeming heritage:

> However secularized our modern civilization may become, this sacred tradition remains like a river in the desert, and a genuine religious education can still use it to irrigate the thirsty lands and to change the face of the

world with the promise of new life. The great obstacle is the failure of Christians themselves to understand the depth of that tradition and the inexhaustible possibilities of new life that it contains.[65]

Rooting Out Discrimination

Catholic teaching concerning the dignity of the human person as grounded in his *being* provides a firm basis for equality and justice. Without this ontological (and hence, eminently realistic) starting point, it becomes inevitable, as history has clearly shown, that the human being will be defined by one or another of his *accidents*. The predictable result of this definition by accident is inequality and discrimination.

This also explains the urgency which John Paul attached to what he referred to as "anthropological realism." We do not know how we should live until we know who we are. This same anthropological realism is crucial if we are ever to realize the discrimination that is currently levelled against the unborn.

Catholic education embraces both philosophy and theology. Her philosophy is a search for truth, including the truth of man. This truth of man in its ontological character is a universal. A universal, naturally, is a generality and as such, though an object of the intellect, is not an object of love. The Church's theology, however, because it is a theology of Christian love, urges people to direct their love toward individual human beings. In this way, philosophy and theology work hand in hand, one supplying the truth, the other, the moral imperative. In this way, also, Catholic education honors both the universal as well as the individual dimensions of the human being.

Godfried Cardinal Daneels, in a collection of essays by various authors under the title, *Handing on the Faith in an Age of Disbelief*, expresses great sympathy for the many people in the world today who are bereft of both truth and love. In this deprived state, he says, they experience both "darkness" and "cold." Many of them seek love, but they look for it apart from truth. "But what good is it to be warm," the Archbishop of Malines-Brussels asks, "if you are in the dark?" "Love is not enough; we need also, and first of all, the truth, without which the fire is but a straw fire." The twin goals of authentic Catholic education are beautifully encapsulated in Psalm 85, line 11: "Kindness and truth shall embrace." The truth can make us free, while love can make us whole.

John Paul II, in *Crossing the Threshold of Hope*, refers to *"the great anthropocentric shift in philosophy"* in which Descartes redefines the human being in terms of consciousness. Referring to St. Thomas Aquinas, John Paul reiterates that "it is not *thought which determines existence, but existence, 'esse,' which determines thought!"* In other words, it is man who thinks, not thinking that is man.

The Cartesian shift away from man's fundamental *being* to an accident (consciousness) took place within philosophy. But this shift, throughout history, has been commonly employed on a practical level. In our own time, Peter Singer, for example, in his book, *Practical Ethics*, rejects ontology and replaces it with the notion of *quality of life*. Thus, he divides humanity into those who do or who do not have what he calls a "preferred state."

The practice of dividing the human race according to some accidental feature and then discriminating against those who occupy the "wrong" side of the spectrum is particularly evident with regard to abortion. There are those who are "unwanted," an accidental feature by which they are arbitrarily labelled as such, and those who are "wanted."

People who are "pro-choice" unwittingly accept this anthropocentric shift as if it were an indication of enlightenment, not suspecting that it is a form of discrimination. Contemporary Americans, however, would do well to familiarize themselves with their own history of discrimination based on this anthropocentric shift. In this regard the history of social Darwinism in America is most instructive, as well as disturbing.

In *The Descent of Man*, Charles Darwin writes: "The advancement of the welfare of mankind is a most intricate problem: all ought to refrain from marriage who cannot avoid abject poverty for their children; for poverty is not only a great evil, but tends to its own increase by leading to recklessness in marriage."

Darwin is not concerned with universal human rights based on a common human nature (nor in helping people to rise from poverty), but in dividing the human race into the wealthy and the poor, or the more fit and the less fit, or the strong and the weak. Such a division, of course, is the form that fuels discrimination. Social Darwinism in America has been amply documented. Richard Hofstadter's *Social Darwinism in American Thought* and Edwin Black's *Eugenics and America's Campaign to Create a Master Race* are well researched and highly recommended.

Social Darwinism in America may have reached its apogee in 1927 in the notorious *Buck v. Bell* Supreme Court decision. This Court, by an 8-1 count, ruled in favour of forcible sterilization. Chief Justice Oliver Wendell Holmes' statement that "Three generations of imbeciles is enough" will reverberate forever.

Neither I.Q. nor economic factors go into determining the humanity of the human being. Yet, we find Justice Blackmun making the following statement in the 1977 *Beal v. Doe* Supreme Court case: "But the cost of a nontherapeutic abortion is far less than the cost of maternity care and delivery, and holds no comparison whatsoever with the welfare costs that will burden the State for the new indigents and their support in the long years ahead." By this strictly economic calculus one could argue in favour of aborting every pregnant woman. In this case, ironically, the economically costly is commensurate with all human beings.

Catholic teaching, both theologically and philosophically, honors all human beings and does not enter the dangerous area of presuming to judge which segment of them are fit to inherit the earth. It is based on a firm foundation in reality and functions as a preventative against all forms of anti-human discrimination.

THE COFFEE SHOP

Good art rings true. The word "ring" is just right because it resonates nicely with the sound of the alarm clock that wakens people to a new day. Unlike the alarm clock, however, good art awakens the somnolent to moral verities. Consider, for example, Picasso's *Guernica* and Michelangelo's masterpiece that decorates the vault of the Sistine Chapel. Good philosophy may be sound, but it may leave people sound asleep. The combination of art and philosophy can not only awaken people, but enables them to smell the coffee.

Art can be prophetic, an early alarm that warns people of approaching storms. The artist, to borrow Ezra Pound's phrase, is the "antennae of the race." He senses certain distortions or contradictions in society and gives them coherent expression before they become widespread. Dostoevsky did not live long enough to see the abominations that he predicted; Solzhenitsyn experienced them first hand.

Edward Hopper painted *Nighthawks* in 1942. It is an icon of anonymity and alienation. The artist himself saw it as an image of "the loneliness of a large city." In the painting, three customers and a counter server are present in a coffee shop late at night when nothing else, apparently, is going on. They are, as one critic remarks, "as remote from each other as they are from the viewer." The shop is painted with no discernable doorway, a somewhat disturbing image that brings to mind Jean Paul Sartre's most celebrated play, *No Exit*, in which three misfits personify Hell as "other people."

The uncommunicative night-owls are frozen in time in what seems to be a sealed environment. They appear to exist without goal or purpose. T. S. Eliot may have captured their mood in his poem "The Love Song of J. Alfred Prufrock" when he wrote, "I have measured out my life with coffee spoons."

The painting conveys a clear moral message: it is not good for human beings to be strangers to each other, to have nothing to do late at night except drink coffee, to inhabit an environment that is devoid of any hint of vitality or cordiality, a place where the only warmth is in the coffee cups. Another critic senses a "menacing air" that haunts the interior of the Coffee Shop.

The Art Institute of Chicago purchased *Nighthawks* not long after it was completed for $3,000. It has remained there ever since. But has it retained its moral force? Unfortunately, in our consumer culture, good art often decays into a cliché. Hopper's most famous work of art has been the subject of endless parody. In one version, Elvis Presley, Marilyn Monroe, James Dean, and Humphrey Bogart inhabit the shop. Another version features cartoon characters. Prints of *Nighthawks* are readily available through the Internet. It is now very much part of the commercial landscape, a tired cliché that has lost much of its original moral force.

The transition from art to cliché results in the weakening of a work of art's moral power. We wonder how that original power can be revived at the present time when it is needed more than ever before. Do we now take anonymity and alienation for granted and no longer see them as aberrations? Have we allowed them, almost without noticing, to enter into the fabric of our everyday lives and even, heaven forbid, into our most sacred precinct of personal intimacy–procreation? Could the stolid environment of Hopper's Coffee Shop in any way be replacing the marriage bed? Such a suggestion sounds utterly fantastical! But a world without moral values is utterly fantastical.

The October 2, 2011 issue of *Newsweek* features an article entitled, "The Coffee Shop." In this instance, the coffee shop remains a scene of anonymity and alienation, but one that has, indeed, become a setting for human procreation. The article draws attention to three coffee shop customers. Two are lesbians who are "married" to each other; the third is a sperm donor. The man enters the bathroom and exits with a sperm-filled latex cup. One of the lesbians takes the cup into the other bathroom and attaches it to her cervix. And then, as writer Tony Dokoupil states, "the three sat down for coffee together." No conception resulted, a non-event that seems to mar the trio's elaborate strategy.

We have given too wide a berth in today's society to anonymity and alienation. With little if any moral realization, we have allowed them to substitute for the fruitful intimacy expressed between husband and wife. In the attempt to make all marital relationships equal (and offend no one in the process), society has unwittingly brought about a radical depreciation of the moral value of conjugal intimacy, and, at the same time, a wholly gratuitous promotion of impersonal and alienated forms of procreation. Two-in-one flesh and one in each public bathroom are now presumed to be equal.

What forms of new art do we need in order to cast a revealing spotlight on the present moral confusion? Can we still rely on the timeless relevance of Shakespeare, Dante, Brueghel, Da Vinci, Beethoven, or Plato? If art does not degenerate into a cliché, it is now routinely deconstructed into a text, purged of any moral significance and as ambiguous as a Rorschach Test inkblot. As University of Leeds professor, Frank Ellis, has complained, "the Bible, Shakespeare, and rap 'music' are just texts with 'equally valid perspectives'." We raise a triumphant banner to equality when we should be writing an epitaph for the death of moral meaning. We have become deconstructed, as C.S. Lewis warned in his 1947 classic, *The Abolition of Man*, into "men without chests." So eviscerated, we may well wonder if we have also become men without hope.

—PART THREE—
THE MEANS FOR FLOURISHING IN A FALLEN WORLD

THE GIFT OF FATHERHOOD

*"If God took the name Father, it was to inspire us with
a greater confidence in him."*

This remark that St. John Vianney delivered to his audience
of farmers in the village of Ars, during his "Sermon of Hope,"
must have seemed to the good Curé one that was entirely free of
controversy. Yet the postmodern world, as we know all too well,
is bent on dissolving this relationship. Fatherhood, whether one is
referring to God, priests, or laymen, is no longer easily and agree-
ably associated with confidence.

In an issue of *American Psychologist* (June 1999), to take
an example from the world of psychology, authors Louise B.
Silverstein and Carl F. Auerbach penned an article entitled, "De-
constructing the Essential Father." "We see the argument that fathers are essential," they write, "as an attempt to reinstate male
dominance by restoring the dominance of the traditional nuclear
family with its contrasting masculine and feminine roles." They
also strongly reject the notion that "fathers are essential to child
well-being, and that heterosexual marriage is the social context in
which responsible fathering is more likely to occur."

In the world of philosophy, the highly influential existentialist Jean-Paul Sartre was unrestrained in his denunciation of father-hood. In his autobiography, *Les mots*, he writes: "There is no good father, that's the rule. Don't lay the blame on man but the bond of paternity, which is rotten . . . Had my father lived, he would have lain on me at full length and would have crushed me." Sartre was awarded the Nobel Prize, according to the Swedish Academy, "for his work which, rich in ideas and filled with the spirit of freedom and the quest for truth, has exerted a far-reaching influence on our age." Sartre's impact was particularly strong among young people who believed that his unfettered view of individual freedom was liberating.

The campaign to deny the essential importance of father-hood (and even eradicate fatherhood itself) is, in a larger sense, nothing new, though the terminology has changed over the years. In today's world, we read about the need to "deconstruct" father-hood, implying that fatherhood is some kind of arbitrary and unim-portant "construction." Psychiatrist David L. Gutmann identifies what he calls the "deculturation" of paternity with "narcissism," a me-first egotism that is hostile not only to any societal goal or larger moral purpose, but also to anything but the most juvenile understanding of personal happiness (*Reclaiming Powers: Men and Women in Later Life*, 1994).

Pope John Paul II, taking a broad view of fatherhood, makes the startling point in his international best-seller, *Crossing the Threshold of Hope*, that Original Sin is "above all" an attempt "to abolish fatherhood." The disobedience of our primal parents was a rejection of God's legitimate authority. But God's authori-ty is inseparable from his fatherly love. Hence, a rejection of his authority was also a rejection of his Fatherhood. John Paul offers a most important insight when he identifies Original Sin with the attempt to abolish fatherhood. The Serpent offers Adam and Eve a caricature of fatherhood – an authoritarian posture that is incom-patible with human freedom.

The first step, then, in restoring the good name and the fullness of fatherhood, is to re-establish the original connection between fatherhood and an identity that inspires confidence. The dissolution of this connection and the resulting state of "fatherlessness" is truly calamitous. David Blankenhorn, for example, provides evidence in his book, *Fatherless America: Confronting Our Most Urgent Problem*, that fatherlessness is the leading cause of the declining well-being of children and the engine that drives our most urgent social problems from crime to adolescent pregnancy to child sexual abuse to domestic violence against women. Despite the massive social problems that fatherlessness has created, he informs us, the concerted effort continues to "deconstruct" and "deculture" paternity.

In his elegant and insightful memoir, *Blessings in Disguise,* Alec Guinness recounts an unintentional experience of fatherhood he had while he was in France for the filming of *Father Brown.* Sir Alec, dressed in priestly black, was traversing a winding road that led to the village where he had a room for the night. He had not gone far before he heard scampering footsteps and a piping voice calling, "*Mon père.*" A young boy of about seven or eight seized the actor's hand, swung it back and forth and kept up a non-stop prattle. Guinness dared not say a word to him for fear that his "excruciating" French would scare him away. Suddenly, with a "*Bonsoir, mon pére,*" and an awkward bow, the boy released his grip and disappeared through a hole in a hedge.

Reflecting on the incident, Guinness began to think more positively about "a Church which could inspire such confidence in a child, making its priests, even when unknown, so easily approachable." Sir Alec's journey home that night was part of a longer journey that ultimately led him into the Catholic Church. Even the portrayal of fatherhood can inspire genuine trust.

Nathaniel Hawthorne had the well-deserved reputation of being a good father and devoted husband. His daughter, Rose, who later came into the Church and, as a Dominican nun, took the name Mother Alphonsa, offers a splendid testimony of her love for her father: "To play a simple game of stones on one of the grey benches in the late afternoon sunshine, with him for courteous opponent, was to feel my eyes, lips, hands, all my being, glow with the fullest human happiness." This is the kind of love for dad that the eminently quotable Adabella Radici captures when she writes: "I love father as the stars – he's a bright shining example and a happy twinkling in my heart."

"I could not point to any need in childhood so strong," wrote Sigmund Freud, "as that for a father's protection." How much do children need a father? As author Maggie Gallagher tells us, "children not only need a father, they long for one, irrationally, with all the undiluted strength of a child's hopeful heart."

The Nobel-Prize-winning novelist, Albert Camus, was killed at the age of 46 in a car crash near Paris in 1960. Near the wreckage, investigators found a black briefcase that contained 144 pages of an autobiographical novel he had been preparing. When it was finally published, 43 years later, it contained these poignant words reflecting how much he lost when his father was killed in the First World War in 1914: "I tried to discover as a child what was right and wrong since no one around could tell me. And now I recognize that everything had abandoned me, that I need someone to show me the way, to blame and praise me... I need a father."

Re-establishing the natural connection between fatherhood and confidence is needed in order to do justice to God, priests, and laymen who have children (either biologically or by adoption). Fatherhood is multi-faceted and organic. It is not simply one thing, such as authority, strength, reproductive achievement, being a breadwinner, or having the legal privilege of passing on one's name. Perhaps worst of all, from the arena of reproductive technology, fatherhood is not merely a "donor" or a "seed." Fatherhood is a paradox, a dynamic blend of opposites, as it were, a fact of life that makes it both indefinable and elusive, on the one hand, but rich and magisterial, on the other.

The following 10 paradoxes illustrate the dynamic quality of fatherhood, a quality that invests it with both vitality and depth.

Fatherhood means being:

1. *An authority without being authoritarian.*

The father, like God, shares in the authorship of life. He is an authority and therefore someone to learn from and be guided by. But his authority does not restrict the liberty of others. In fact, the purpose of fatherly authority is to cultivate and enhance liberty. St. Thomas Aquinas wisely pointed out that "the respect that one has for the rule flows naturally from the respect one has for the person who gave it" (*Ex reverentia praecipientis procedere debet ex reverentia praecepti*). A person best understands fatherhood by knowing someone who is a good father. One must begin with the real experience and not a cultural caricature.

2. *A leader without being a frontrunner.*

Our prevailing notion of leader comes from the worlds of sports and from politics. In relation to the "leader board" in golf, the leader is the one who is ahead of the rest of the field. In the world of politics he is the one who is leading in the political polls by getting more votes than his rivals. But a father is not a leader in this way. He does not try to remove himself from his family. Nor does he regard the members of his family as rivals. On the contrary, he leads in a manner that fulfills each member. His leadership is inseparable from those he leads. What he leads and "fathers" into being is the good of those whom he loves. In other words, fatherhood requires that a father leads by *being there*, rather than being "ahead of the pack."

3. *A visionary without being arrogant.*

Every home must have a *hearth* and a *horizon*, as Hans Urs Von Balthasar has stated. The father is a visionary in the sense that he has an eye on the future. He has a keen sense of the importance of time. But he has this without presumption or arrogance. He is providential in his fathering. He knows instinctively that his children will grow up and lead independent lives. He provides for them a future vision of themselves and works hard to make that future a reality.

4. *A servant without being servile.*

The expression *"servus servorum Dei,"* adopted by John Paul II, comes from Pope Gregory the Great. Paradoxically, this servant of the servants of God earned the appellation "Great." "He who humbles himself shall be exalted." The father serves all the members of his family without being in any sense subservient or inferior. One might say, in this respect, that fathers, like tennis players, enjoy an *advantage* when they serve.

5. *A lover without being sentimental.*

The love of a father is strong and unwavering. His love is not bound by a feeling, and hence prone to sentimentality. It is strengthened by principles that always focus on the good of others. Love means doing what is in the best interest of others. In this regard, authentic love can be "tough love." Sentimentality means always being nice because one is fearful of criticism. The real father has a spine and is not afraid of whatever opinions others may have.

6. *A supporter without being subordinate.*

A father is supportive. He holds people up, keeps them going when they are inclined to be discouraged. But his encouraging role does not imply subordination, but the kind of reliability and trustworthiness that one can expect from someone who is strong. He is not supportive in the Hollywood sense of being a "supporting actor." His supportive role is played out, as a matter of fact, as the leading man.

7. *A disciplinarian without being punitive.*

A good father knows the value of rules and the consequences of disregarding them. He wants his children to be strong in virtue. Therefore, he knows the importance of discipline, restraint, and self-possession. He is not punitive, nor is he overbearing. He makes it clear to his children that there is no true freedom without discipline, and that discipline requires training. He is wary of punishment as such, since it can strike fear in the heart of a child.

8. *Merciful without being spineless.*

Mercy must be grounded in justice. Otherwise it is dissipation and weakness. In fact, mercy that disregards justice is unjust. A father, because he recognizes the uncompromisable importance of justice is anything but heartless. He is merciful, but his mercy perfects his justice. Mercy without justice is mere capitulation to the desires of others. Justice without mercy is cold legalism.

9. *Humble without being self-deprecating.*

Humility is based on the honest recognition of who one is and the nature of one's role. It takes into account one's limitations and weaknesses. The humble father, when he encounters difficulties, has enough humility to ask for help, even at times, from his own children. Yet, he never gets down on himself. He knows that remaining self-deprecating at a time of crisis is utterly futile. He has the heart to help and the humility to enlist the help of others.

10. *Courageous without being foolhardy.*

Courage is not fearlessness, but the ability to rise above fear so that one can do what needs to be done in a time of danger or difficulty. A father does not fall apart when he begins to feel the pressure. Foolhardiness is not courage but an unfocussed and unhelpful recklessness. Moreover, courage, as its etymology suggests, requires heart. The father, above all, is a man of heart.

Fatherhood, on all these levels, should inspire us with confidence. The child takes the hand of his father, the communicant receives the Eucharist from the priest, the believer prays to "Our Father who art in heaven." The rupture between fatherhood and confidence can he healed and restored to its original wholeness. St. John Vianney has reminded us that fatherhood and confidence go together. His simple and wise words, spoken almost in obscurity, have more truth in them than what can be found among all the postmodern thinkers who are vainly trying to deconstruct fatherhood on every level. God the Father will not be mocked; the Serpent will not be triumphant.

> *"Think of the love that the Father has lavished on us by letting us be called God's children and that is what we are"* (1 Jn 3:1). *"We are children of God by adoption. By the gift of the Holy Spirit we are able to cry 'Abba, Father"* (Ga 4:6).

THE GIFT OF MOTHERHOOD

William Butler Yeats, who knew a great deal about poetry, though perhaps very little of theology, once remarked that "The rhetorician would deceive his neighbors, / The sentimentalist himself; while art is but a vision of reality." Poetry, as a form of art, does offer a "vision of reality" and one that lies between these two common forms of deception. When it is poetry in the best sense, it offers us glimpses into reality that we can ill afford to do without. Science, opinion polls, psychological theories, and the like, are but shadows in comparison with the light by which poetry can illuminate certain realities.

G. K. Chesterton, who was more comfortable than Yeats with the intersection of poetry and theology, maintained that "great poets use the telescope as well as the microscope." This paradoxical feature may make great poets obscure for opposite reasons, he said: "because they are talking about something too large for anyone to understand, and now again because they are talking about something too small for anyone to see."

Such is the poetry of motherhood, for the mother sees something real in her child that others either do not see or cannot see nearly as well, and because she senses the far-ranging implications of the effects of her mothering. She applies both the microscope and the telescope to her child. It is altogether fitting, then, that John Henry Cardinal Newman would call the Church herself, *Ecclesia*, "the most sacred and august of poets." The Church, like the mother, has a vision that is both sacramental as well as poetic. Each understands the eternal implications of the passing moment as well as the infinite potential that lies within an unpretentious parcel of flesh.

Hans Urs von Balthasar, one of the most insightful and prolific Catholic theologians of our time, opens Volume III of his *Explorations in Theology* with this beautiful and thought provoking sentence: "The little child awakens to self-consciousness through being addressed by the love of his mother."

It is precisely because of this moment of utterly unselfish love that the poet Samuel Taylor Coleridge referred to motherhood as "the holiest of all things." In this image of the "I" of the child awakening in response to his mother's loving smile, theology and poetry coincide. Van Balthasar elaborates on this coincidence when he says that: "the child does not 'consider' whether it will reply with love or nonlove to its mother's inviting smile, for just as the sun entices forth green growth, so does love awaken love; it is in this movement toward the 'Thou' that the 'I' becomes aware of itself. By giving itself, it experiences *I* give *myself*. By crossing over from itself into what is other than itself, into the open world that offers it space, it experiences its freedom, its knowledge, its being as spirit."

God left to motherhood the task of being an indispensable aid in the final crossing from what appears to be mere life to that being's vital awareness that he is far more than that – a subject, a conscious I who is destined to love and live in a wide and challenging world. No true mother, intimately involved as she is in completing the creative order, can be an atheist.

The generosity of the mother's love has its corollary in the relative undevelopment of the child she loves. Added to her generosity, therefore, is an extraordinary sensitivity to human potential. John Paul II, himself both a theologian and a poet, once wrote:

> Mother of the Incarnate Word!
> You are the human heart's immaculate sensitivity
> To all that is of God . . .

Mary is the model of all motherhood. We find this special "sensitivity" praised in Gerard Manley Hopkins' poem, "The May Magnificat":

> All things rising, all things sizing
> Mary sees, sympathizing
> With that world of good
> Nature's motherhood.

This uncanny sensitivity a mother has for her infant has been noted by the distinguished philosopher and Nobel Laureate, Henri Bergson. In this book, *The Two Sources of Morality and Religion*, he turns the reader's attention to the special sensibility the mother has for her child, something that he believes is "supra-intellectual in that it becomes divination": "How many things rise up in the vision of a mother as she gazes in wonder upon her little one? Illusion perhaps! This is not certain. Let us rather say that reality is big with possibilities, and that the mother sees in the child not only what he will become, but also what he would become, if he were not obliged, at every step in his life, to choose and therefore to exclude."

The mother divines in her child things that non-mothers apparently cannot. She is both a seer and a prophet. This special quality is as indispensable to the human race as is her ability to give birth. We know from various psychological reports about the debilitating effects the absence of a mother's love has on infants.

A British poet by the name of Anne Ridler (1912-2001), who at one time served as a secretary for T. S. Eliot, authored 11 volumes of poetry over a 50-year span. Herself, mother to two sons and as many daughters, she has penned a number of poems that reveal her own acute sensitivity to the mother-child relationship. In *Choosing a Name*, she beautifully expresses the motherly paradox we find when generous love embraces gossamer child:

> Strong vessel of peace, and plenty promised,
> Into whose unsounded depths I pour
> This alien power;
> Frail vessel, launched with a shawl for sail,
> Whose guiding spirit keeps his needle-quivering
> Poise between trust and terror,
> And stares amazed to find himself alive;
> This is the means by which you say I am,
> Not to be lost till all is lost,

Here, mother's love parallels God's creative love where He lifts us out of nothingness. God reaches out to us in our nothingness. The mother's reach extends to her child's apparent near-nothingness. Hence, the holiness and extraordinary generosity and prescience of motherhood.

Elsewhere, Ridler reflects that motherly vision in which she sees the eternal implications of the fleeting moment:

> Life beating with secret purpose;
> What I see face to face,
> Is recognition,
> Spark of the eternal light.

In a poem entitled, "A Mother to Her Waking Infant," Joanna Baillie (1762-1851) returns to the theme that von Balthasar identified above, involving the loving mother addressing her child who is slowly awakening to consciousness of himself:

> Now in thy dazzling half-oped eye,
> Thy curled nose and lip awry,
> Thy up-hoist arms and noddling head,
> And little chin with chrystal spread,
> Poor helpless thing! What do I see,
> That I should sing of thee?

> From thy poor tongue no accents come,
> Which can but rub thy toothless gum;
> Small understanding boasts thy face,
> Thy shapeless limbs nor step nor grace;
> A few short words thy feats may tell,
> And yet I love thee well . . .

Here, Ballie is not expressing a sentimental view of motherhood, but a sacred wonder that is inseparably linked to a poetic and realistic vision of the child she loved. Lord Byron saw enough realism in Baillie's poetry to put her on a par with Sir Walter Scott and Thomas Moore.

Lastly, we turn to the personality and poetry of Anna Laetitia Barbauld (1743-1825). A child prodigy, she could read before she reached the age of 3 and was soon thereafter fluent in French and Italian. She subsequently became proficient in Latin and Greek. Her first book of poetry, published when she was 30, earned wide acclaim. She won the praise of both Coleridge and Wordsworth.

In one poem, with the elongated title, "To a Little Invisible Being Who Is Expected Soon to Become Visible," she addresses the child in the womb:

> Come, reap thy rich inheritance of love!

Bask in the fondness of a Mother's eye!
Nor wit nor eloquence her heart shall move
Like the first accents of thy feeble cry.

Haste, little captive, burst thy prison doors!
Launch on the living world, and spring to light!
Nature for thee displays her various stores,
Opens her thousand inlets of delight.

Yeats warned, as we noted at the outset, of the deceptions associated with sentimentalism and rhetoric. It would be sentimental to depict motherhood as all sweetness and light, devoid of burdens, dilemmas, worries and woes. Surely, nothing could be more unsentimental than the frequency of diaper changes. Let us not deny that a mother's work can be, at times, drudgery. But Chesterton cautions us about the double meaning of that word: "If drudgery only means dreadfully hard work, I admit the woman dredges in the home." But a mother's work is not drudgery, he added, "because it is trifling, colorless and of small import to the soul."

The fact that a mother's work is difficult does not prevent her vision of the child from being poetic, and even theological. Nor does it deny that her office is monumental. The eternal implications of the diamond in her wedding ring still glimmer during diaper changes. The trials that Christ bore did not mar his mystical capacities. Unsentimentalism and mysticism are not only compatible, they are actually complementary.

Yeats also warned us about deceptive rhetoric. Unpoetic, unmotherly (even anti-motherly) rhetoricians have persuaded countless people that motherhood is merely a "choice." Yet, to vaporize motherhood into a whim represents the greatest of all deceptions. As philosopher Peter Kreeft has put it, "Motherhood with a capital M [is] a metaphysical force of which human mothers are but mere carriers. Her vocation speaks with authority – an absolute, and imperative, a divine revelation."

Motherhood helps to keep poetry alive, incarnating it into something undeniably real and decisively fruitful. At the same time, poetry — the validation of important realities that happen to be unmeasurable—helps to keep the true nature of motherhood alive.

Poetry, as we have stated, is situated between two deceptions. The tragic deception in the current era is the reduction of motherhood to a choice. This reduction is concurrent with the popular trend in literary criticism to deconstruct poetry into meaninglessness. At this juncture of human history, Mary, the model of motherhood, becomes all the more indispensable.

CAN IMMUNOLOGY
CORROBORATE *GENESIS*?

Our immune system, certainly one of the great marvels of nature, equips us with 100 billion (100,000,000,000) immunological receptors. Each of these tiny receptors has the uncanny natural capacity to distinguish the *self* from the *nonself*.[66] Consequently, they are able to immunize or protect our bodies against the invasion of foreign substances that could be harmful to us.[67]

Marvelous as nature is, it is never extremist. From a purely immunological point of view (from the standpoint of an all out defensive strategy), a woman's body would reject the oncoming sperm, recognizing it as a foreign substance. But this is precisely the point at whic nature, we might say, becomes wise. If our immune system regards sperm as a potential enemy, then fertilization would never take place, and the human race would have come to an early demise with the passing of Adam and Eve.

But something extraordinary occurs that makes fertilization and the continuation of the human race possible. Traveling alongside the sperm in the male's seminal fluid is a mild immunosuppressant. Immunologists refer to it as consisting of "immunoregulatory macromolecules." This immunosuppressant is a chemical signal to the woman's body that allows it to recognize the sperm not as a *nonself*, but as part of her own *self*. It makes possible, despite the immune system's usual preoccupation with building an airtight defense system, a *self*-to-*self* union or, from an immunological perspective, a "two-in-one-flesh" intimacy.

The male semen carries spermatozoa that have the capacity to fuse with the nucleus of the woman's egg (fertilization). In addition, it carries a mild immunosupressant that allows the woman's immune system to welcome the male sperm as part of her own flesh. Nature is congenial to heterosexual procreativity.

With regard to sodomy, on the other hand, a pertinent question can be raised: What happens when semen is deposited in the rectal area rather than in the vaginal tract? How do the spermatozoa and the immunosuppressant function when they are placed in this particular bodily environment?

1.   Male sperm, being unresponsive to political ideologies or cultural trends, behave strictly according to their nature. They penetrate the nucleus of whatever body cell (somatic cell) they might encounter. This fusing, however, does not result in fertilization, the first stage in the life of a new human being, but, as scientists have observed, can and does result in the development of cancerous malignancies. In an article entitled, "Sexual Behaviour and Increased Anal Cancer," authors Richard J. Ablin and Rachel Stein-Werblowsky, report that "anal intercourse is one of the primary factors in the development of cancer."[68] They make the following observations:

a.   Spermatozoa are capable of penetrating somatic cells and fuse with their nuclei.

b.   Nuclear fusion, other than in normal fertilization, can result in malignant transformation in the invaded tissue.

c.   Immunoregulatory macromolecules may directly and/or indirectly contribute to an immunopermssive environment favourable for the perpetuation of spermatozoa (or otherwise)-induced tumours and/or be a factor for tumorigenic-associated infectious agents.[68]

Daling et al., writing for the *New England Journal of Medicine*, states: "Our study lends strong support to the hypothesis that homosexual behaviour in men increases the risk of anal cancer."[70] In addition, Melbye *et al.*, reporting in the *International Journal of Cancer* finds that "Being single and having practiced anal intercourse appears to be associated with anal cancer and case reports have suggested a recent increase in the number of cases of anal cancer."[71] The medical literature on this point is extensive.

2.   Scientists have confirmed that when the male immunosuppressant is deposited in the rectal area an "immunopermissive environment" is created. This environment, in which the immune system is not working as it should, is favorable for the perpetration of spermatozoa-induced tumors and other pathologies. It is as if, in this instance, the immune system becomes confused and welcomes its enemies. Researchers have documented a decreasing immunocompetence in a substantial proportion of HIV-positive homosexual men, particularly those with a history of intraepithelial abnormalities.[72] It has been shown in a number of studies that, unlike all sexually transmitted diseases, where both partners are equally susceptible to the disease, in homosexual males, immunosuppression appears in the anal sperm recipients but not in the partners who deposit the sperm.[73]

Depositing sperm in the "wrong place" (like pouring motor oil into the gas line), by nature's standards, is courting disaster. Nature, we might add, demands respect. It does not make accommodations to politically based ideologies or individual preferences. This is a point that Dr. Jeffrey Satinover makes throughout his book, *Homosexuality and the Politics of Truth*.[74] From nature's standpoint, there is no equality between heterosexual and male homosexual intercourse.

Furthermore, the vagina is totally impermeable to viruses. By contrast, the rectum is designed to absorb up to the last possible useful nutrient that we have eaten. There is an enormous lymphatic network (involving blood vessels) in the lining or mucosa of the rectum. Therefore, the rectal area is designed to absorb, and will absorb the ingredients of male semen if they are in the vicinity.[75]

One researcher states that "The risk of anal cancer soars for those engaging in anal intercourse. According to one report, it rises by an astounding 4,000%, and doubles again for those who are HIV positive."[76] Despite the well documented adverse medical consequences associated with sodomy, this damaging practice is strongly supported. Indeed, even the Supreme Court (in *Lawrence et al. vs. Texas*, June 26, 2003) has specifically upheld male to male sodomy. According to Justice Anthony Kennedy, writing for the Majority, "Persons in a homosexual relationship may seek autonomy for these purposes {The right to define one's own concept of existence, of meaning, of the universe},[77] just as heterosexual persons do." In dissent, Justice Antonin Scalia saw the *Lawrence* decision as allowing politics to usurp law: "Today's opinion is the product of a Court, which is the product of a law-profession culture, that has largely signed on to the so-called homosexual agenda, by which I mean the agenda promoted by some homosexual activists directed at eliminating the moral opprobrium that has traditionally attached to homosexual conduct."

Science in itself, like nature, is immune to political or fashionable trends. Politicians and lawyers, however, are more vulnerable to the seductions of the Zeitgeist. But in looking closely and carefully at what the science of immunology can tell us about the natural functioning of spermatozoa and the male immunosuppressant, we have even more reason for upholding and honoring the wisdom of marriage as the potentially procreative union of a man and a woman. In this regard, we have added reason to feel awe when we re-read the passage in the first chapter of *Genesis* that refers to marriage as a union of "two-in-one flesh." Immunology gives us reason to believe that this phrase is not a mere metaphor, but is descriptive of a reality unique to the conjugal bond between a man and a woman.

Immunology, of course, does not tell us what marriage is. But it does underscore the radical importance of the body and the fundamental importance for life of the distinctiveness of the sexes. On the other hand, Al and Tipper Gore's book, *Joined at the Heart* (2002), to take but one example among many that represent a growing trend,[78] by employing a metaphor, fails to appreciate the corporeal solidity of marriage. It is difficult to see how, by missing what is elementary to marriage, one could properly appreciate the subsequent psychological, spiritual, personal, and religious levels of marriage for which the body has prototypic significance.

Immunology corroborates the notion of the "two-in one-flesh" meaning of marriage as recorded in *Genesis* on a scientific level. It offers yet another example of the compatibility of science and faith.

THE POWER OF VIRTUE

We usually think of justice as rendering what is due to another ("*Justitia est ad alterum*," in the words of St. Thomas Aquinas). In this sense, we see justice as a virtue that has an interpersonal nature. It is also possible to view justice as rendering what is due to something that is not a person. In this sense, a singer, for example, can "do justice" to a musical selection, or a reviewer can do justice to the book he is reviewing. We can also do justice to an idea. We do justice to the notion of virtue when we speak of it properly in the fullness of its meaning.

Doing justice to the notion of virtue is important not only because of the critical importance of virtue in the moral life, but also to distinguish true virtue from the many counterfeit and aberrant notions of virtue that are rampant in culture. For many people, virtue is like a kaleidoscope which, as it is turned, displays an intriguing array of variations on the theme of virtue, but not virtue itself in its undiluted and undistorted truth. Doing justice to virtue, then, is doing justice to truth.

1. Virtue as Harmful:

Friedrich Nietzsche dedicated a good portion of his life to

railing against Christian virtues, especially those he thought were feminine, such as chastity, modesty, meekness, and pity. Such virtues, for Nietzsche, were actually harmful since they prevented the emergence of the "Superman" (übermensch).

In *The Will to Power*, Nietzsche argues that the pity by which a person is moved to assist someone who is weak or suffering, is "more dangerous than any vice." "Virtue is our greatest misunderstanding," he writes. In his view, "One should respect fatality – that fatality that says to the weak: perish!"

Nietzsche, despite his patent misanthropy, has never lacked for admirers and imitators in the modern world. Ayn Rand is a good example of a thoroughly Nietzschean devotee. In declaring that "Altruism is the root of all evil," and that "Money is the barometer of a society's virtue," she is professing her philosophical kinship with Nietzschean morality.

Someone who at least comes close to saying that *money* is the root of all good is the cinematic character played by Michael Douglas in the move *Wall Street*. Gordon Gecko is a Wall Street bandit who addresses an assembly of stockholders. His solution for their company, Teldar Paper, is to "save" it by "downsizing it." In a style that is truly mesmerizing, Gecko pontificates as follows:

> Greed, for lack of a better word, is good. Greed is right. Greed works. Greed clarifies, cuts through and captures the essence of the evolutionary spirit. Greed, in all of its forms—greed for life, for money, for love, knowledge—has marked the upward surge, and greed, you mark my words, will not only save Teldar Paper, but that other malfunctioning corporation called the USA.

Gecko's panegyric to greed, on the other side of the coin, is his denunciation of generosity. Virtue, in the traditional sense, reaches out to the weak; greed, formerly a Deadly Sin, is now a source of life. "Woe to him who mistakes vice for virtue," warned Confucius (and *vice versa* we might add). At the end of the move, Gordon Gecko becomes an inmate in a Federal Prison, which seems to be the logical and inevitable result of his dubious thinking and double-dealing. *Wall Street*, therefore, is a morality play that reveals, slowly but convincingly, what Dostoevsky showed in *Crime and Punishment*, namely, that the wages of sin are not higher wages, but either death or personal disintegration.

2. Virtue as Uncool:

"I used to be Snow White, but I drifted." This phrase is attributed to Mae West. Whether it was her own brainchild or that of one of her many writers, is beside the point. The phrase captured her lifestyle. Ms. West was, as they say, a woman of "easy virtue." If something is too easy, it usually does not exemplify what it is supposed to be. Wine that ages for a month is not a vintage wine. "Character," as Goethe once said, "is formed in the stormy billows of the world." The shortcut is the quickest route to nowhere. Neither virtue nor life itself is easy.

Mae West's depiction of herself is not only amusing, but engaging. She makes sexual promiscuity appear "cool," and, by contrast, makes chastity seem "uncool." "Chastity is its own punishment," it is said. Alex Comfort, who made a fortune selling licentiousness, (his hastily-written 1972 book *The Joy of Sex* earned him worldwide fame and $3 million), was more forthright and less amusing when he said, "We might as well make up our minds that chastity is no more a virtue than malnutrition."

It is considered "uncool" to be chaste. When football star Tim Tebow declared that he was saving himself for marriage, he provoked a tidal wave of ridicule. While many supported him, many of Tebow's peers thought it was just too "uncool" to be celibate before marriage. Many of Tebow's critics find a lot of other virtues to be "uncool," such as patience, modesty, meekness, graciousness, and courtesy.

Being "cool" is not being virtuous. It is a curious substitute for virtue. It is largely an attitude, one that fears being pretentious, avoids hard work, and craves the approval of others. It is catering to the IN crowd and distancing oneself from the "old fogeys" of the world. But it is the stance of the immature person. The distinctions between what is "cool" and what is "uncool," between what is "hot" and what is not, between what is IN and what is OUT are grossly inadequate replacements for "right" and "wrong," "good" and "evil." Real virtue is more concerned about loving others than being admired by them. Elvis Presley was cool, but his inner life was in turmoil.

James Bond, 007, is super-cool. He is detached, imperturbable, supremely confident, and emotionally unavailable. He has been a role model for those who find it easier to be aloof than to be in love. The cool person, presumably, never gets emotionally scarred. But if this is true, it is only because he does not truly care about anyone other than himself. He is never truly in love. Consider the following words of C. S. Lewis: "There is no safe investment. To love at all is to be vulnerable. Love anything, and your heart will certainly be wrung and possibly be broken. If you want to make sure of keeping it intact, you must give your heart to no one, not even an animal. Wrap it carefully round with hobbies and little luxuries; avoid all entanglements; lock it up safe in the casket or coffin of your selfishness. But in that casket — safe, dark, motionless, airless — it will change. It will not be broken; it will become unbreakable, impenetrable, irredeemable." It is not cool to be passionate, but it is not redeemable to be cool.

3. Virtue as Unnecessary:

"All you need is love," sang the Beatles. It was an appealing notion, because it excused people from the arduous and time-consuming task of cultivating virtues. Psychiatrist Bruno Bettelheim (1903-1990) offered a more realistic view of love in his book, *Love is Not Enough* (1950). Though this noted psychiatrist had his own problems, his notion that love is a practical concern rather than just some amorphous good feeling, is eternally valid.

Love may represent good intentions, but as Canadian novelist Margaret Atwood has confessed, "My good intentions are completely lethal." We know that Hell is paved with good intentions, though this does not imply that Heaven is paved with bad intentions. Love is practical concern. It is deed. It is the will to do good. But love does not cross over into doing good for someone in the absence of virtue.

A fire department analogy may be of help at this point. Water puts out fire. Water represents a supply of love; the fire represents someone in distress who needs love. But there must be an intermediary to bring the water to the fire (or love to where it is needed). This, of course, is the hose. Virtue is the hose, so to speak, or the conduit that brings love to the person loved. It is the connective that transmits love in a practical and beneficial way. If a man declares his love for a woman, but lacks chastity, temperance, patience, and other important virtues, he is a pathetic soap opera character whose love, if it is there at all, is stillborn. The unvirtuous suitor does not need a woman as much as he needs a character makeover. Virtue is necessary if love is to be delivered. When unvirtuous people prey upon each other, tragedy is the inevitable outcome. The shallow soap operas may be entertaining, but they are seldom instructive. Jean-Paul Sartre's celebrated phrase, "Hell is other people," is an accurate description, but applies only to an assemblage of unvirtuous people.

Love without virtue is sentimentality. Love focuses on the other person; sentimentality focuses on the feeling in the self. Love is a tendency toward reality, but needs virtue to get there.

124

Love is the power, virtue is the delivery system. Virtue is as necessary to love as musical instruments are to music. Tolstoy tells of aristocratic ladies who would shed tears over the troubles that theater actors portray on the stage, while serenely oblivious to their coachmen who are waiting for them outside in the freezing cold.

4. Virtue as a Mask:

In Book II of his Republic, Plato tells the story of the Ring of Gyges which gives its possessor the power to be invisible. In the dialogue, Plato has Socrates and Glaucon engaged in a dispute concerning virtue. Socrates contends that virtue is truly personal and does not depend on what others may think or on a fear of being caught. Glaucon disagrees with Socrates and insists that people act morally only because they fear reprisals. If someone had the Ring of Gyges, which rendered him invisible, he would see no need of being virtuous and would enjoy a very profitable immoral life. Hence, Glaucon believes that virtue is just a mask of social respectability.

A recent survey posted on the Internet asked husbands and wives if they would cheat on each other if they were assured of not being caught. 30% of the men and 16% of the women responded in the affirmative. These potential cheaters take the position of Glaucon. But their willingness to engage in infidelity (if the price was right) does not call into question the virtue of the majority of men and women whose commitment to fidelity is truly personal and irrevocable. Vice does not cast virtue in doubt. Rather, as Francois La Rochefoucauld famously said, "Hypocrisy is the tribute that vice pays to virtue."

The often heard moral maxim, "Crime does not pay" represents the Socratic position that committing a crime, even though one is not caught, poisons the soul of the criminal. Virtue is good for others as a way in which love is expressed, but it is also good for the virtuous person inasmuch as it strengthens his own soul and helps him to achieve authenticity as a moral person. The person who practices unvirtuous acts is faced with the tribunal of himself. He cannot escape his own realization of the iniquity of his actions.

St. Ambrose, in his commentary on the Ring of Gyges rejects the cynical position of Glaucon and affirms that even "if an upright man could hide himself, yet he would avoid sin just as though he could not conceal himself; and that he would not hide his person by putting on a ring, but his life by putting on Christ." We cannot escape getting caught by our own conscience whenever we commit an unvirtuous act. St. Ambrose concludes that we should therefore not let expediency get the better of virtue, but, like the "upright man," regard virtue as superior to expediency.

Maintaining a mask of virtue is not easy. "Do you not know," Kierkegaard asks, "that there comes a midnight hour when everyone has to throw off his mask? Do you believe that life will always let itself be mocked?" Nathaniel Hawthorne would have agreed with the Danish existentialist: "No man can, for any considerable time, wear one face to himself, and another to the multitude, without finally getting bewildered as to which is the true one."

5. Virtue as Proof of Being a Self:

In the preface of the book version of his immensely successful play, *A Man for All Seasons*, Robert Bolt, asks himself why he chose St. Thomas More to be his subject: "Why do I take for my hero a man who brings about his own death because he can't put his hand on an old black book and tell an ordinary lie?" Samuel Johnson had said of Thomas More that "he was the person of the greatest virtue these islands ever produced." Bolt greatly admired More for the virtue he exemplified as a genuine expression of who he is. He was "a man," writes Bolt, "with an adamantine sense of his own self."

When a person makes a vow, he declares who he is. He binds himself through his word to a certain virtuous conduct. It is all too common for people to take vows lightly, to break them when they prove demanding or ignore them whenever it is convenient. A man makes a vow, writes Robert Bolt, "when he wants to make an identity between the truth of it and his own virtue; he offers himself as a guarantee." In the play, More refuses to give in to the king, to perjure himself and betray his Church. "I will not give in because *I* oppose it – *I* do – not my pride, nor my spleen, nor any other of my appetites but *I* do – *I*." There is no dissociation between More's being and his life. Dostoevsky appropriately named the main character in his *Crime and Punishment* "Raskolnikov" because *raskol*, in Russian, means "divided."

Only a person of integrity, which is to say, of virtue, is capable of making a genuine vow. He must have the moral strength, as well as the freedom, to ensure that his solemn word is not a frivolity but a steel cable that binds himself irrevocably with his actions. True virtue is evidence of a whole person. It is a person's identity, his commitment to be himself.

Cynics may take virtue lightly because they take vows even more lightly. They view virtue not as the soul's possession, but as an advantageous social ornament. The vow, however, should be taken as seriously as the self and should be prized as much as virtue. This is how the inimitable G. K. Chesterton expresses it:

> The vow is to the man what the song is to the bird . . . It is not easy to mention anything on which the enormous apparatus of human life can be said to depend. But if it depends on anything, it is on this frail cord, flung from the forgotten hills of yesterday to the invisible mountains of tomorrow.

Vows not only unite the person with his life, but generations with generations. Virtue, therefore, which the vow presupposes, unites persons, people, nations, and generations. Virtue is, indeed, the property of the soul. But even more than that, virtue is at the core of social justice.

6. Virtue as an Expression of Love:

According to St. Thomas Aquinas, "love is not only a virtue, but the most powerful of virtues." Indeed, for the Angelic Doctor, love is "the form of all virtues" (*De Caritate* a. 3; *Sum. Theol.* II-II, q. 23, a. 8). Each virtue, therefore, derives its virtuousness by virtue of its relationship with love. Love, then, acts as an efficient cause, thereby directing all virtues. For this reason, Aquinas refers to love as "the mother of the other virtues."

It may seem that any act which produces good may be called virtuous, but as Aquinas maintains, "no strictly true virtue is possible without charity." Aquinas, as well as St. Augustine (cf. *Contra Julian* iv, 3) were careful to distinguish between true virtues, rooted in love, and counterfeit virtues that did not spring from love. "The prudence of the miser," Aquinas states, "is no true prudence; nor the miser's justice whereby he scorns the property of another through fear of severe punishment; nor the miser's temperance, whereby he curbs his desire for expensive pleasures" (*Summa. Theol.* Q. 23, a 7).

—Conclusion—

True virtue is the expression of a loving person, directed toward some benefit for another person. It is at once, loving and personal. It is not, as we have tried to show, something that is harmful, something that is controlled by fashion, a superfluity, an arbitrary social amenity, or a mask we are forced to adopt in order to save face. When we do justice to the notion of virtue, we see it precisely as it is in its truth: a salutary power that is rooted in love and expressed through the person for the benefit of other human beings. Moreover, it is twice blessed and lies at the core of social justice.

Is Laughter Juvenile or Rejuvenating?

Ecclesiastes 3:4 tells us that there is "a time to weep and a time to laugh." In so stating, we are reminded that life is not monochromatic. It is varied, like a symphony, in mood and texture. In addition, it calls us to be attentive to the real encounters that life arranges for us. We weep for a lost loved one; we laugh over our human foibles.

The word "time" is also of particular interest. It can refer to specific circumstances that strike us as laughable. Or, it can refer to a period of time. The latter is the meaning of time for a recent survey on laughter conducted in Britain.

According to this survey, infants laugh up to 300 times a day. This rate plummets sharply for teenagers to six times a day. The rate continues to drop as life goes on: 4 daily laughs for those in their twenties, 3 for people in their fifties, and a paltry 2.5 for sexagenarians.

The time to laugh seems to be when we are very young. Yet, *Ecclesiastes* may be suggesting that something is wrong here. Laughter should not be compartmentalized by age, but limited only by the number of occurrences that we find hilarious.

Nova Scotian humorist, Thomas C. Haliburton maintains that "God has made sunny spots in the heart," and questions "why we should exclude the light from them?" For Haliburton, humor should transcend age barriers. After all, it is associated with a condition of the heart that God has fashioned in all of us. Moreover, laughter is something we need. If worry is a weight, then laughter is a counterweight, the former being gravity, the latter being levity. According to *Proverbs* 17:22, "A cheerful heart is good medicine." This simple wisdom has been repeatedly verified scientifically. Laughter reduces stress, strengthens the immune system, is an invaluable exercise for a number of internal organs, and releases endorphins – the body's natural pain-reducing agents. "Frame your mind with mirth," Shakespeare advised, "which bars a thousand harms and lengthens life." "Laughter," wrote Victor Hugo, "is the sun that drives winter from the human face."

Why is it, then, that we make diminishing use of laughter as life goes on and, even, perhaps, as our need for it increases? Dostoevsky sheds important light on this matter when he describes the laughter of children. "Children," he writes, "are the only creatures to produce perfect laughter and that's just what makes them so enchanting . . . a laughing child is a sunbeam from paradise for me, a revelation of future bliss when man will finally become as pure and simple-hearted as a babe."

The great novelist is saying that while laughter is better identified with children, it is not restricted to them, that we may one day re-acquire the simple-heartedness of the child. Laughter, in any of us, may well be a moment when we are free from all anxieties and experience a delightful foretaste of that day in paradise when there will be no worry to taint our joy. "Let the children come to me, and do not hinder them," Christ recommended, "for such belongs to the kingdom of heaven. Truly, I say to you, whoever does not receive the kingdom of God like a child shall not enter it" (Luke 18: 16-7). Raoul Plus, S.J., author of *Christ in Our Time*, readily imagines Christ laughing when children came to him, climbed on his lap, tweaked his beard, and simply enjoyed his fatherly companionship. As we age, we should be approaching heaven rather than drawing away from it.

We can remain childlike, while out-growing childishness, by retaining the simplicity of a child that prevents us from taking life so seriously that it keeps us from laughing. Scripture is advising us to age without growing old, to see the humor in everyday foibles and the folly of our own vanity. We do not remain youthful by laughing, but we laugh because we have found the secret of staying young at heart. And the secret of staying young, of remaining a child, is preserving that simplicity of heart which allows us to see the moments of joviality that enter our lives. It is not juvenile to laugh, but it can rejuvenate the child in us. G. K. Chesterton has famously stated that "Satan fell by the force of gravity," whereas "Angels can fly because they take themselves lightly."

The British survey acknowledged that the laughter rate of people in their thirties increased. It credited this rise to parental involvement with their children. Laughter is infectious. It is a testimony to our communal nature. It is enjoyable, therapeutic, memorable, and, yes, even Godly.

LOVE AND THE HUMAN FACE

During his homily in a Mass at St. Peter's for the feast of Mary, Mother of God, Pope Benedict XVI offered the world a most thought-provoking reflection on peace. This subject, of course, is most appropriate for the first day of the year since January 1 marks the annual celebration of the World Day of Peace.

The Pontiff developed the point, perhaps original in its application, that peace begins when we look upon the face of the other person. This looking upon the face of another, as Benedict was careful to explain, will find the "depth" of the human face "only if we have God in our hearts." Then, he stated, "we are in a condition to detect in the face of others a brother in humanity — not a means, but an end, not a rival or an enemy, but another 'I,' a facet of the infinite mystery of the human being." The face as essentially human transcends ethnicity, race, gender, and social status.

One who has an "empty heart," on the other hand, perceives nothing more in other faces than "flat images." But the more we are inhabited by God, the more sensitive we are to "his presence" in others. Hence, the significance of a common Father who loves us all despite our weaknesses and limitations. In looking into the face of another, one can experience the unveiling of the face of

God.

In the case of Mary looking upon the face of her Son, we have a prototype — or an **icon** — of one person seeing the face of God in another. Benedict stated: "She who guarded in her heart the secret of divine maternity was the first to see the face of God made man in the tiny fruit of her womb." Conversely, the first face that a child sees is that of his mother and it is this gaze that "is decisive for his relationship with God. It is decisive as well so that he can become a 'child of peace'."

The face *speaks*. It speaks of love and is the beginning of all subsequent discourse. The mother's face is like the face of God for her baby. Looking into her face, the infant comes to believe that the world outside the womb is safe and trustworthy. The child picks up these messages intuitively and immediately as it studies the face of his loving mother.

In a world of widespread depersonalization, in which people move about side by side rather than face to face, a reflection on the profound significance of the human face is critically needed. In pornography, for example, as psychiatrist Leslie Farber and others have pointed out, the fig leaf is transferred to cover the face. In this transference, the impersonal gains ascendancy over the personal. It also signifies a suppression of the spiritual.

The great, Russian Orthodox philosopher, Nikolai Berdyaev, like Benedict, understood how the spiritual order can manifest itself in the human face. In *Slavery and Freedom* he writes: "The face of man is the summit of the cosmic process, the greatest of its offspring, but it cannot be the offspring of cosmic forces only, it presupposes the action of a spiritual force, which raises it above the sphere of the forces of nature. The face of man is the most amazing thing in the life of the world; another world shines through it. It is the entrance of personality into the world process, with its uniqueness, its singleness, its unrepeatability."

Darwinian evolution cannot begin to explain the emergence

in the cosmos of the face as a bearer of the spiritual. For Darwin and his disciples, the spiritual realm exists wholly outside of their limited sphere of discussion concerning physical variations and chance mutations. As the noted geneticist Theodosius Dobzhansky has pointed out, human beings properly belong to an "ethical," not a "gladiatorial" mode of existence. The "ethical" is not something that evolves from matter.

Returning to Benedict XVI's homily, the Holy Father acknowledges that the human face can also be marked by the harshness of life and by the effect of evil. But "the faces of innocent little ones are a silent call to us to take responsibility: Before their helplessness, all of the false justifications for war and violence come crashing down." The face carries a plea to defend and protect.

Pope Benedict then draws a connection between respect for the person and protecting the environment: "If the person is degraded, the environment is degraded; if culture tends to nihilism — if not in theory, then in practice — nature cannot fail to pay the consequences." There is a reciprocal relationship, therefore, between the face of the person and the face of the environment. The distorted visages of emaciated children are directly connected to an environment that has not served them justly or properly.

The call to justice is written in the face of the human person, though it takes a godly person to see this. Those who argue that religion has been history's leading cause of violence and warfare fail to recognize this primordial fact. The Judeo-Christian tradition clearly, repeatedly, and consistently reminds its disciples that a refutation of war is written in the human face. War is unjust, and peace is not possible without justice. Consequently, peace begins when one sees the inscription in the face of the other not to kill and, by honoring that inscription, renders him justice.

Pope Benedict, by connecting the human face with the "face" of the environment, is offering an integrated vision, one in which philosophy, theology, ethics, and care for the environment are all blended together in a consistent and meaningful pattern. His January 1, 2010 homily has profound, realistic, and rich implications for the whole world at a most critical time.

CONCLUSION

We are inescapably *finite freedom*. We are free not because we can fly, but because our feet are on the ground.

We are not exempt from the pains and tribulations that rise from our mortality. Nor are we entirely free from our own inherent weaknesses.

The prospect of death gives our life meaning because it gives value to every moment of our existence. We do not have an eternity of time to become the persons we are destined to be. Anthony Burgess' words, taken from his *Confessions*, are worth pondering: "Wedged as we are between two eternities of idleness, there is no excuse for being idle now."

Our own weaknesses necessitate the cultivation of virtue. We need the courage "to be" in the face of all the difficulties and threats that life poses. How else, but in a world of challenges can a soul be roused to action and become truly itself?

Within the narrow limits of time, space and individual capacity, a human being can flourish. At the same time, one must avoid the heresies that our will should never be restricted, our society is perfectible, that pleasure is paramount, and that adversity is meaningless. No matter how much the world has fallen, we can find reasons for hope. "The times are never so bad," wrote Saint

Thomas More, "that a good man can't live in them." And let us not underestimate the importance of a single act of kindness. As Portia remarks in *The Merchant of Venice*, "How far that little candle throws his beams! So shines a good deed in a naughty world."

We can flourish in a fallen world by taking advantage of the many gifts that are available to us while living within the truth of our being. That truth, though set in a finite context and subject to innumerable trials, gives us the power to be open, through knowledge and love, to the Infinite. It allows us to be open and receptive to the God Who made us and Who wills that we do far more than merely subsist, but that we flourish.

ENDNOTES

[1] Plato, *Republic III*, 409c, tr. Paul Shorey.

[2] Plato, *Carmides*, 157a-b, tr. Benjamin Jowett.

[3] Norman Cousins, *Head First: the Biology of Hope* (E. P. Dutton: New York, NY, 1989), p. 281.

[4] Plato, *Symposium*, 187a, tr. Michael Joyce.

[5] Plato, *Phaedo*, 118, tr. Hugh Tredennick.

[6] J. W. Provonsha, "The Healing Christ," *Current Medical Digest*, December, 1959, p. 3.

[7] Morton T. Kelsey, *Healing and Christianity* (Augsburg Books: Minneapolis, MN, 1995), p. 51.

[8] *Ibid.*

[9] St. Augustine, *Sermones Novi Testamenti*, Sermo CCXXXI, tr. Benedict Groeschel, CFR.

[10] *Ibid.*, pp. 41-54.

[11] Meredith O'Brien, "The Rescuing Hug: The Benefits of Co-Bedding Infant Twins," www. my-happy-heart.com.

[12] Daniel E. Koshland, Jr., "Recognizing Self from Nonself," *Science*, Vol. 248, No. 4961, June 15, 1990, p. 1273. "When the immune system is working well it never gets activated by self substances, but unerringly responds to the nonself substances. When the system is not working well this distinction gets blurred and diseases of autoimmunity occur."

[13] Cousins, Op. *cit.*, p. 287.

[14] Viktor Frankl, *Psychotherapy and Existentialism: Selected Papers on Logotherapy* (Simon and Schuster: New York, NY, 1967), pp. 43, 67, 76, 122, 183, 209, 217.

[15] St. Thomas Aquinas, *Summa Theologica*, I-II, 38, 3.

[16] Op. *cit.*, I-II, 32, 5.

[17] Arthur Schopenhauer, *The World as Will and Idea*, trans. R. B. Haldane and J. Kemp (London: K. Paul, Trench, Truber, 1906), 2:354.

[18] *Ibid.*

[19] *Ibid.*, p. 219.

[20] *The Living Thought of Schopenhauer* (London: Cassell, 1939), p. 28.

[21] Karl Stern, *The Flight From Woman* (New York, NY: Farrar, Straus, & Giroux, 1965), p. 22.

[22] Cornelio Fabro, *God in Exile: Modern Atheism*, tr. by Arthur Gibson New York, NY: (Newman Press, 1968), p. 872.

[23] Judith Jarvis Thomson, "A Defense of Abortion," in *The Rights and Wrongs of Abortion*, eds. M. Cohen et al. (Princeton, N.J.: Princeton University Press, 1974), p.3.

[24] John T. Wilcox, "Nature As Demonic," *The New Scholasticism*, Vol. LXIII, Winter 1989, p. 475.

[25] *Ibid.* p. 475.

[26] Quoted in Robert Payne, *Marx* (New York: Simon & Schuster, 1968), p. 192.

[27] Auguste Comte, *Catéchisme positive* (Paris: Garniér, 1890), p. 39.

[28] Auguste Comte, *Lettres inédites à C. de Blignières* (Paris: Vrin, 1932), pp. 35-36.

[29] Peter Singer, *Rethinking Life and Death: The Collapse of Our Traditional Ethic* (New York: St. Martin's Press, 1995).

[30] Derek Humphry, *San Francisco Chronicle*, August 28, 1972.

[31] Rita Marker, *Deadly Compassion* (New York: William Morrow, 1993), p. 166.

[32] Peter Singer, *Practical Ethics* (Cambridge: Cambridge University Press, 1979), p. 331.

[33] George Weigel, *Witness to Hope* (New York: HarperCollins, 1999), p. 334.

[34] Agnosticism literally means, "knowing nothing."

[35] Etienne Gilson, *Reason and Revelation* (New York: Charles Scribner's Sons, 1938), p. 71.

[36] Joseph Cardinal Ratzinger, *Truth and Tolerance: Christian Belief and World Religions*, trans. Henry Taylor (San Francisco: Ignatius Press, 2004), p. 84.

[37] *Ibid*, p. 3.

[38] *Ibid*, p. 10.

[39] *On Divination*, pp148-9.

[40] Mortimer J. Adler, *Truth in Religion: The Plurality of Religions and the Unity of Truth*, p. 128.

[41] Pope Benedict XVI and Marcello Pera, *Without Roots: The West, Relativism, Christianity, Islam*, trans. Michael F. Moore (New York: Basic Books, 2006), p. 87. On page 33 Pera writes: "Relativism has wreaked havoc, and it continues to act as a mirror

and an echo chamber for the dark mood that has fallen over the West. It has paralyzed the West, when it is already disoriented and at a standstill, rendered it defenseless when it is already reluctant to rise to the challenge."

[42] *Ibid*, p. 88.

[43] Jacques Maritain, *On the Use of Philosophy: Three Essays* (New York: Atheneum, 1965), p. 24.

[44] See G. K. Chesterton, *The Everlasting Man* (Garden City, NY: Doubleday & Company, 1960), p. 231.

[45] Allan Bloom, *The Closing of the American Mind* (New York: Simon Schuster, Inc., 1987), p. 25.

[46] *Ibid*.

[47] *Time*, September 10, 1979, p. 69, Frances Fitzgerald writes: "All of us children of the twentieth century know or should know that there are no absolutes in human affairs."

[48] Albert Einstein, *The World as I See It* (New York: Covici-Friede, 1934), p. 60

[49] See Stanley L. Jaki, *The Absolute Beneath the Relative* (Lanham, MD: University Press of America, 1988), pp. 1-22.

[50] Mortimer J. Adler, *How To Read A Book* (New York: Simon and Schuster, 1940), pp. 366-67.

[51] Benedict XVI, "The Natural Law is the Basis of Democracy," October 5, 2007 (Zenit.org).

[52] Pera and Ratzinger, *op. cit.*, p. 117.

[53] Gordon W. Allport, *The Nature of Prejudice* (Garden City, NY: Doubleday & Company, 1958, p. 477.

[54] *Ibid.*

[55] Benedict XVI, op. *cit.*

[56] Jacques Maritain, *The Rights of Man and Natural Law* (New York: Charles Scribner's Sons, 1947), p. 60.

[57] *Ibid*, p. 61.

[58] *Summa Theologica*, I, Q. 41, 1.

[59] Benedict, *op. cit.*

[60] *Dignitatis Humanae* 14.

[61] *Evangelium Vitae* 11.

[62] Joseph Cardinal Ratzinger, *On the Way to Jesus Christ*, trans. Michael J. Moore (San Francisco: Ignatius Press, 2002), p. 45.

[63] *Ibid*, p. 100.

[64] George Weigel, *Witness to Hope* (New York: HarperCollins, 1999), p. 334.

[65] Christopher Dawson, *Understanding Europe* (New York: Sheed & Ward, 1952), p. 255.

[66] Daniel E. Koshland, Jr., "Recognition of Self from Nonself." *Science*, June 1 5, 1990: 1273.

[67] F. M. Burnet, "Immunological Recognition of Self: Such recognition suggests a relationship with processes through which functional integrity is maintained." Science, Feb. 3, 1961, 133: 307-311.

[68] *Immunology and Cell Biology*, 75: 1997, 181-83.

[69] *Ibid.*, p. 182.

[70] J.R. Daling, N.S. Weiss, J. A. Ryan, L. Corey, R.J. Coates, K.J.

Sherman, R.L. Ashley, & M. Beagrie, "Sexual Practices, Sexually Transmitted Diseases, and the Incidence of Anal Cancer." *New England Journal of Medicine*, 16; 1987: 937-73.

[71] M. Melbye, *et al.*, "Immune Status as a Determinant of Human Paillomavirus Detection and its Association with Anal Epithelial Abnormalities, *International Journal of Cancer*, 46: 1990: 203-06.

[72] M. Melbye, C. Rabkin, M. Frisch, R.J. Biggar, "Changing patterns of anal cancer incidence in the United States, 1940-1989. *American Journal of Epidemiology*, 1994: 139: 777-80.

[73] G. M. Maviigit, *et al.* "Chronic immune stimulation by sperm alloantigens," *JAMA* 251: i984: 237.

[74] Hamewith/Baker Books, 1996.

[75] T.C. Quinn, *et al.* "The Polymicro Origin of Intestinal Infections in Homosexual Men." *New England Journal of Medicine*. 1983: 309: 573-82. William, D. C. *et al.*, "Sexually Transmitted Enteric Pathogens in Male Homosexual Population. *New York State Journal of Medicine*. Nov. 1977: 2050-51.

[76] Melonakos, MA, RN, "Why Isn't Homosexuality Considered a Disorder On The Basis Of Its Medical Consequences?" NARTH, May 15, 2004: 2.

[77] Here, Justice Kennedy is quoting himself (in brackets) from *Planned Parenthood vs. Casey*, 1992.

[78] I offer two but examples here: 1) Andrea O'Reilly, ed., *Mother Outlaws: Theories and Practices of Empowerment Mothering* (Toronto, ON: Women's Press, 2004), p. 126 where the author extols the "new" family in which "gendered demarcation and embodiment is {sic} forever displaced." 2) Margaret A. Farley, *Just*

Love: A framework for Christian Sexual Ethics (New York, NY: Continuum, 2006), p. 288: ." . . the justice ethic appropriate to heterosexual relationships is the same justice ethic appropriate to same-sex relationships."

www.ingramcontent.com/pod-product-compliance
Lightning Source LLC
Chambersburg PA
CBHW022010090426
42741CB00007B/969